Enjoy my Book

# DON'T WAIT FOR THE TOOTH FAIRY

How to communicate effectively and create the
perfect patient journey in your dental practice

*Ashley Latter*

authorHOUSE®

*AuthorHouse™ UK*
*1663 Liberty Drive*
*Bloomington, IN 47403  USA*
*www.authorhouse.co.uk*
*Phone: 0800.197.4150*

*Published by AuthorHouse    05/01/2015*

*ISBN: 978-1-4520-8884-6 (sc)*
*ISBN: 978-1-4969-9808-8 (e)*

# What people are saying about Ashley Latter

I attended Ashley's Ethical Sales and Communication Programme about six years ago. Initially I was a bit sceptical about having to travel to Manchester but apart from needing to buy an extra jumper it was excellent. It stretched me out of my comfort zone and made me break down why and how people make decisions. The two days seemed to drift by. When I came back to the practice I realised my whole team needed to do it so arranged to close the practice for a day and Ashley came to London to train them as well. It was worth every penny and I would encourage not just dentists but all the team to attend. It will stretch you, make you think and see the power of understanding why patients come to see us and how we can help them make responsible decisions about caring for their mouths.

**James Goolnik Dentist, Bow Lane Dental and author of Brush - Amazon number 1 in Dentistry.**


I just wanted to take the time to say thank you from the bottom of my heart.

I have attended countless hours of education on all aspects of dentistry and have been unable to deliver the care due to my inability to communicate effectively with patients. When I did communicate I found myself uncomfortable talking about fees.

I should have taken your course first. I made a mistake! Now I can start to practice the dentistry I love and even having been back at work one day, the skills I have learnt have already made a positive impact on my practice.

I may have mentioned this to you already, but I do not consider you a good teacher. In fact, I don't consider you to be a teacher at all. Teachers 'drill' information into you, and you did not do this. You are a world class LEADER, and this came over in your course. You demonstrated knowledge, integrity and an innovative style which only makes me regret not taking your course sooner.

I would go beyond recommending your course and stating that if anyone is serious in delivering quality dentistry, your course should be as important as learning the advanced principles of dentistry.

**Pav Khaira, Red Sky Dental Spa**

It was great to meet you all and I thoroughly enjoyed the course. The enthusiasm you show Ashley is infectious and is just the thing to spur me on.

Next day I was 'Lattering' my patients and signed up just over £5000 worth of investment with a phase 2 plan for one of the patients which will be in the region of £12-14,000!

I am excited about the process and it is fun to apply it and a challenge.

Will sort out the advanced course and keep the momentum going. The best of luck to all my fellow course attenders.

Thanks Ashley.
**Peter Workman, Affinity Dental Care**

Every person in our practice has had Ashley's training. His training is part of our culture every day when we communicate with clients
**Gayna Horridge, Treatment Coordinator, Cahill Dental Care Centre**


Thank you for delivering the Two Day Ethical Selling Course. For months I had been deliberating whether or not I should go on the course. I finally decided enough was enough and booked onto it... I was certainly not disappointed.

Your positive attitude and genuine character made it really easy to absorb the information over the two days. I now see patient communication in a whole different light and that's down to you. The proof is in the pudding, and the first day back in the practice I was able to ethically sell £1000's of private work, I can't believe it! I've made my money back from the course and will be definitely reinvesting!

The course has made me realise that communication is the key to building strong relationships with patients. I truly now believe that the patient should benefit from the product more than the dentist.

I love the fact that I have a structure to my conversation flow and that I am confident in talking about money with patients.

For anyone that is deliberating on going on the course, DONT. Ashley is a genuine person that knows exactly how to empower you so that you can perform to your potential. I am finally able to provide the treatment that I enjoy.
**Dr Adeel Ali, Hermitage Clinic**

I attended your ethical sales programme in November and just wanted to email you and say thank you for all the help and advice you gave me. I was fairly new to the TCO role and was struggling to discuss money and close my appointments but since your course I'm doing so much better! It didn't happen overnight but gradually we are getting some really good results and feedback, this month I have seen 17 new patients and 15 have booked in for treatment plans so needless to say the boss is happy too!

I will be recommending your course to anyone who asks and we are also looking into booking our receptionist in on the reception course,
**Rachel Worth, Treatment Coordinator, Diana Dental**


Hi Ashley,

I hope you are well. I just wanted to pass my gratitude for the excellent training my newest Treatment Coordinator Zhara received from you recently. Within a week she has repaid the course fee five times over.

I know my staff (future and present) will continue to benefit from your courses in the future.

Thanks again

**Mark Skimming**
**Dentistry on the Square, Glasgow**

As time passes by I am beginning to reflect on my 17 year dental career and I can identify key turning points in my career pathway which have allowed me to prosper and feel a true sense of personal fulfillment from dentistry.

One of those key turning points was when I attended your Two Day Ethical Selling Course 9 years ago at Gatwick. I had followed your articles in the dental press for a while and had listened to your audio CD titled "The Tooth Fairy" many times and I felt I needed to attend your course to help me, at the time, in my transition from an NHS clinic to a fully private one.

Without a doubt your course had a major impact on my self-perception, my personal confidence and my ability to communicate with patients about my dentistry and to educate them on the benefits my care could offer them.

When I returned to my clinic I applied your principles and I have never looked back. Today my clinic has flourished into an award-winning high profile cosmetic dental clinic in London's West End and all your principles still form a major part of the way I communicate with patients. In fact, over the years I have sent any new team members to your Reception and Treatment Co-ordinator courses so they can also benefit from your training.

When I reflect back and think what I may have spent to attend your course I can sincerely say that the investment is totally irrelevant as my production revenue has grown by more than 500% over the years largely due to the confidence and communication skills you taught me.

From the bottom of my heart I would like to thank you and I look forward to sending any new team members to you in the future as I know they will get the very best communication training.

**Anoop Maini, Aqua Dental Clinic**

Thank you for running your programme a few weeks ago to my Implant Group. The feedback we have received has been absolutely fantastic and life changing. I knew it would. On a personal level I have now taken your programme five times and I learn more and more every time I take your course. I wished I had known about you when I left Dental School

**Stephen Jacobs, Owner Dental FX**

"I highly recommend the Ethical Sales and Communication course to anyone looking to increase turnover and profitability in their practice. Over the last 12 months we've had an eight fold increase in the take up of Invisalign treatments. On one open day alone we converted 20 enquiries from patients who actually went into Invisalign treatment. The return on investment has been substantial. Can't recommend it enough"

**Tirj Gidda, Principal Dentist, Omnia Dental Spa**

I personally took Ashley's programme for the first time in 1999 and since then I have taken his programmes virtually every year. Without doubt his programmes are the most important and profitable courses you can take. 90% of our success in the surgery comes down to communication & the relationships we form with our patients. We were not taught these skills at Dental School. It is the missing link. There is not a day goes by when I am not using Ashley's principles in the surgery and I personally know that his principles are

responsible for hundreds of thousands of pounds worth of extra treatment during this period.
**Neil Sampson, Newcastle Dental Implant Clinic**

I went on Ashley's course over two years ago and only now have decided to write a testimonial! Why? Because I wanted to road test what I learnt thoroughly before revealing my experiences.

Ashley has not only increased my sales significantly but improved my confidence and comfort in discussing treatment plans with patients, and as a consequence my relationship with patients is more relaxed and positive.

Dental professionals I feel have mastered the art of teeth but not the art of sales when it comes to what patients want to hear. I used to over complicate explanations and essentially talk patients out of having treatment by making it sound daunting. Ashley's classic question of 'do you have any concerns' still fascinates me with the responses I get. The old me would have listed to the patients concerns that they hadn't even thought of and basically frightened them away!

I now use his sales method verbatim including the bits that some people could deem embarrassing such as asking for testimonials and recommending friends. The beauty of a set pattern for a consultation is that you come across as confident and professional and as such allows you to focus on the patients' needs and concerns without you having to think 'what shall I say next?'

Thank you Ashley for a whole new perspective on patient management. I knew you had an influence when nurses would say to me 'don't do your own thing with this next patient, you ramble too much. Ashley Latter them'

**Best regards,**
**Tom Crandon, The Orthodontic Centre, Cardiff**


I work in a busy implant practice and I delayed going on Ashley Latter's course for about a year after it was first suggested by a friend that I would find it useful. I came up with all kinds of excuses like I couldn't afford either the time or the money. Oh boy, was I wrong!

It's now been almost 3 months since I took his 2-day ethical sales course and my practising life has changed dramatically; My conversion rates for treatments have soared and January was our busiest month EVER in terms of treatments. But even more than this, I have MORE time. I know this sounds strange - how can I be busier than ever and still have more time? - but it's because I don't spend so long telling patients about the minutia of their treatments. I used to think my long-winded explanations were important, but Ashley made me realise that most patients neither want or need the amount of information I was giving.

Don't make the same mistake I did - book onto Ashley's course NOW - not tomorrow or next week, but NOW. Not only will it save you the fortune in treatments that you are currently missing out on, but it will dramatically improve your working life.

**Bill Schaeffer, The Implant Centre**

It is important that when giving advice to your patients that it is in conjunction with informed consent.

"Informed consent is a legal procedure to ensure that a patient or client knows all of the risks and costs involved in a treatment. The elements of informed consent include informing the client of the nature of the treatment, possible alternative treatments, and the potential risks and benefits of the treatment.

In order for informed consent to be considered valid, the client must be competent and the consent should be given voluntarily".

Legal Notices and Limit of Liability: While all attempts have been made to provide effective and verifiable information in this product, the author and publisher assume NO responsibility for any errors, inaccuracies, or omissions, nor is any liability assumed for ANY damages resulting from the use of the information contained inside, or the ideas implied or derived from this information.

This product is ultimately designed for educational purposes only. It is sold with this understanding, and the understanding that the author and publisher are not engaged in rendering any kind of legal, accounting, and regulatory, compliance or other professional services. If legal advice or other expert assistance is required, you must seek out the services of competent professionals in this area.

# Contents

Grace, Martina, Enrica, Ashley (Me)

# Dedication

I could not write this book without mentioning my internal and most important customers, my wife Graziella (often known as Grace) and my two wonderful children, Enrica and Martina.

It is 2015 and we have been married now for 18 years. A big thanks for allowing me to do what I love. I am often away 80-90 nights a year and you very rarely complain. You are with me all the way and are a true partner. You always ask how the programmes are going and offer superb support back at our base. You have created a wonderful home and I still get excited when I walk through our front door. You have done a brilliant job of bringing the kids up, especially when I am away so much of the time.

Enrica, you are my big girl. You are growing up into a mature young lady and you are looking more beautiful every day. You obviously get your looks from your gorgeous mother. I am so proud of what you are achieving at school and I cannot help you with your homework anymore as you now know more than me. I love my long walks with you and our dog Sandy, down the nature trail and in the park where we live, as you tell me what you are up to and your plans and goals for the future.

Martina, there isn't a nicer sight than seeing you run down the stairs and jump all over me after I have been away on a business trip. It is often worth being away for a few days just to experience one of your long hugs. I love my long chats before you go to bed and playing the yes/no game. I also love your long letters that you send to me and your mum and the beautiful pictures you draw me all the time. Please do not stop drawing these pictures; I want to cover my whole office with them.

You three are my best friends and I am always thinking of you all every day - you are my heroes.

I would also like to thank my fellow Mancunian Chris Barrow for being such a good supporter of my programmes and for being a good mate. We have had many laughs over the last 20 years and it is a privilege to count you as a close friend.

Neil Sampson and Barry Oulton for being the first ever dentists to take my courses, many years ago. How ahead of the game you guys were. Neil, I am proud to say that your family and mine are close friends.

To all my clients who have taken my courses and for the kind words and encouragement you have given me on this crazy journey. You sometimes frustrate the hell out of me, but I am privileged to now count many of you as dear friends.

**Ashley Latter**

# Foreword

I'm delighted that Ashley has invited me to contribute an introduction to his book.

The usual ramble is that we met in the mid-90's, enjoyed the relationship both personally and professionally and have swapped clients ever since.

This is a matter of record – in fact I was in the audience when "Ash" presented that first fateful workshop back in 1997, two dentists attended and were immediately blown away by his material and delivery.

Not being overly stupid, I saw the potential straight away and encouraged Ash to develop his dental services. I'll claim 1% of the praise for his success though – because I've rarely met anybody who works so hard to build his business and look after his clients.

I like to think that Ash and I share four characteristics:

- Original material
- Total commitment
- An inability to please everyone, leading to divided opinion and
- A lifetime of support for the same football club and love for the same town

The first quality is very important for readers of this book.

It's sometimes depressing to see trainers, consultants and coaches rolling out their predecessors and peers material, without attribution. Ash and I call them "cut and paste merchants".

The good news is that what you are about to read here is the real deal, home grown and fired in the furnaces of Mr Latter's busy life and extraordinary 18 years of helping dental teams become better communicators.

The second quality should lead you to seek his services after you read this book.

Ash and I share a similar lifestyle – countless hours of travel and endless nights in hotels.

I recall a telephone call one evening from Ash that went something like this:

Ash: "Hi Chris, where are you?"

CB: "In a hotel in Edinburgh – where are you?"

Ash: "In a hotel in Slough. Can I ask you a question Chris?"

CB: "Fire away."

Ash: "Let me paint the picture. I'm sat in the hotel bar with a pint and a sandwich the night before my workshop. There is nobody else here except the barman. It's my birthday. I miss my wife and daughters. Do you think we are doing the right thing?"

And, of course, we were – to build a business you have to make sacrifices – and every now and then keeping a promise to a client over-rides all else – but as long as you keep things in balance it will be fine.

Making sacrifices yourself also entitles you to ask the same of your clients – to move them out of their comfort zones in order to grow – Ashley is one of the best I've ever seen at doing that respectfully.

I have never known Ash to take his foot off the pedal of total commitment – to his work, his clients – and also to his family, where he is constantly an example to all solo entrepreneurs, including me.

The third quality indicates that there are some sections of this book that will challenge you and your core values. In that, you will duplicate the emotions of the (literally) thousands who have heard Ashley's message over the years and resisted, avoided, dismissed his philosophy. Come to this book with an open mind and you will not be disappointed. You might not even like Ashley's communication or writing style – but see past that and you will uncover a treasure trove of ideas that can transform your career.

Our fourth shared quality will appeal to few – all things Mancunian and especially the famous Man United football club. We are both working class lads who have done well for ourselves, against the odds.

That allows me to say that I think of Ash as a kind of distant professional brother and we always look out for each other. There have been some late night phone calls from me to him.

One of my calendar highlights is our annual pre-Christmas dinner, when we take our respective ladies for a nice meal and chat about the year just gone and the year ahead. Ask Ash himself what happened at our Christmas "do" in 2009 – quite amazing!

It's been a pleasure to have Ash as a constant and true friend for many years – if you are meeting him for the first time in these pages, make sure that you invest a lifetime in getting to know him. If like me, you already do – you know what I mean.

**Chris Barrow**

# Are you in SALES?

I have been asking this question to audiences of dentists all over the UK and Europe for the last 18 years. At the start I would see around 10% of the audience actually put their hands up, now in 2015, it is around 60%. How times have changed. So how do you currently feel about selling? The fact that you are reading this book, tells me that you are in the 60% of dentists who now see these skills paramount to your success.

Well, maybe you don't see yourself as a salesperson; after all you spent over 7 years learning about dentistry, not communication or business skills. In fact, I often hear dentists tell me that it is criminal that they are not taught communication skills at Dentistry School. However, every day, everybody in your practice is selling an idea to another human being. The first person a patient communicates with is the receptionist. In my opinion they are the most important person in your practice. They can have a massive impact on your practice profits, based on how they deal with a patient. They can often make or break whether a patient comes through your door or not. I have written a whole section on the role of the receptionist and how to make your reception area more profitable. The receptionist is also the first person the patient communicates with when they walk through the door. Then there is the Practice Manager who spends all day selling an idea to the team, or to the patient. Probably one of their biggest frustrations is convincing team members to take action on your ideas.

The dentist is always selling an idea to the patient, whether you are discussing a treatment plan, or trying to influence a patient to change their behaviour. Whether the patient takes up your treatment plan or not will depend on how well you communicate your ideas, or, in a lot of cases, don't. Often the patient will ask the advice of the nurse, as she escorts the patient to the desk, so they are also part of the selling process. Last, but not least, the hygienist is selling to patients every day. By the way, if you have an issue with patients not turning up to the hygienist appointment, it is probably because they have not been sold well. For example, if you tell your patient they need to go to the hygienist because they will give you a scale and polish or just clean your teeth; this is not a great incentive to go. More about this later.

Everyone within your team is selling an idea every day to someone. If you are not convincing and not speaking the language of the person you are communicating with, they probably will not buy into your ideas. You all work as a team, just like my favourite team Manchester United, the most successful team in England for the last 20 years. The reason for Manchester United's success is quite simple. They have world class forwards, midfield players, defenders and, of course, a world class goal keeper. You cannot be champions with weak links. That is the same in your practice. For example, I have been told many times by dentists that the patient has agreed to a treatment plan, only to go to the desk to be talked out of it by the receptionist. The baton has been dropped and you now you have a "Sales Prevention Officer" in your ranks. For this very reason, over the last 10 years I have noticed a trend for dentists to bring their whole team to my courses. They do not want the baton dropped by anyone in their practice.

World class communication skills are probably the most important skills you can develop. After all, if you are in private practice, it could be that 100% of your income will derive from your ability to influence patients. With less money going into the NHS, the end of PRSI funding in Ireland and the uncertainty of the economy, these skills may be paramount if your practice is going to survive.

The demand for cosmetic dentistry is growing as the general public want to look 10 years younger and they see a nice smile as a way of making this happen. They have the money to spend and they are keen buyers prepared to shop around for dental services.

Many studies have been done about what makes a person successful. In fact, here is a simple exercise. Think about a person who you know who is successful in dentistry and make a list of all the skills and attributes that person has. Once you have done this, divide them into skills, attitudes and product knowledge. I bet on the list there are many skills such as good communication and listening skills, and the ability to build empathy with the patient. On the attitudes side, are there things like positivity and enthusiasm? Have you also got product knowledge? On occasions, when I have a discussion with a dentist, the technical skills are often left out. Although important, if not vital, the technical skills of doing the job only usually account for about 10-15% of a person's success. Without good communication skills and the ability to build empathy and gain patient commitment, you might never be able to put into practice your technical ability. However, many dentists think that the more technical knowledge they accumulate and pass on to the patient, then the more the patient will become interested. Technical knowledge is crucial; however, it only plays a small part in the sales process.

This was highlighted last year. A dentist from Glasgow brought his whole team to my programme in Manchester. There were eight team members and they stayed for two nights in a hotel in Manchester, so they made a considerable investment of both time and money. At the end of the course he was delighted with the new skills that he had learnt, but he also was visibly upset. It turns out he had learned about my programme three years previously and had been advised then to take it. He was kicking himself at all the opportunities he had missed in that time!

## So why is there negative thinking towards sales?

There is so much misconception about sales and/or selling. It reminds me of the story of the rabbit and the snake who bump into each other in the forest. The snake asks the rabbit who he was, as he was blind and could not see. The rabbit did not know who he was, because he was also blind and could not see. They agreed to touch each other and let each other know who they were. So the snake started to touch the rabbit and stated that he was furry, had a bushy tail and floppy ears. He told him that he was a rabbit. The rabbit was delighted and started hopping around. Then he started to touch the snake, and told the snake that he was smooth, had sharp fangs and a forked tongue, so he was a salesperson. Now, I know that maybe the perception of salespeople has changed, but there is still plenty of bad press for sales which gives it a poor reputation.

Take our national media. It seems that whenever we see something in the news about selling, it is about an unscrupulous salesperson conning vulnerable people. It often involves someone being sold something that they didn't want, or finding what they were sold was not what they were expecting. We tend to associate sales with an unsolicited phone call to you at home, or pushy car salesmen. I often think this is unfair, as it is only a very small percentage that gives the many millions of good sales people a bad name. If you think about it, without the ability to communicate well, the whole country would come to a halt and nothing would ever get made. Business would stop and industry would close down for good.

Today, I discovered that my printers had gone into administration and were closing down. I used these printers for my manuals and brochures and was a good customer for them. I was obviously disappointed and showed a lot of empathy as their work has always been pretty good and I had a good relationship with them. I asked them why they had gone out of business and they informed me it was lack of sales. On reflection, I was not surprised. During my 5 year relationship with them, never once did they ever visit me to find out what I did and ask questions about my business. If they had, they may have made more sales. For example, it is only now that I realise that they did pens, bags, banners and other related products that I could have bought for my business. I may have done 30% more business with them. They also never once asked me for a referral.

With the assumption that sales is about pushing something on a customer when they don't really want it, it is hardly surprising that when I ask the question, 40% of the room never consider themselves in sales. However, as I have already stated, I honestly believe it is less than 1% of the business community that gives sales a bad name.

## What is the definition of sales?

A dictionary definition will tell you that sales is the exchange of goods and services for money or equivalent to convince of value.

There is nothing in the definition that states that it is about pushing people or forcing people into decisions. Let us look at another key word here - value. I think value is finding out what the true value is to the other person in their situation. So, what about changing your mindset from one of selling, or pushing, to:

- Building relationships with the right type of patient
- Finding out what the patient thinks is value (wants and needs)
- You showing how you can help the patient, when he believes you can, that person will probably buy

Think about how you can change your mindset. Look inside yourself and ask what is stopping you? If you think you provide significant value to patients, then why not give more patients the opportunity to enjoy the same services? You are doing them, and yourself, a disservice if you don't. Pay attention to what you are saying to yourself, such as "can't", or "won't" and change to "can" and "will". Change your mindset to: "I provide significant value every day to patients", and read some of the letters that you receive from happy patients.

Your job, and your team's jobs, exists because of your ability and your team's ability to communicate well and influence patients, and, if you think about it, without these skills, your practice would probably not exist.

Sales are something to be proud of. Without your ability to communicate well and listen with empathy, patients will not get what they need, and, in most cases, want, and no one benefits. It is something to be proud of, when done right, both parties benefit.

## Why is this book important?

Over the last 18 years, I have personally trained and coached over 8,000 delegates on my two-day Ethical Sales & Communication Programme. I am proud of the fact that my courses are probably one of the best attended business courses relating to dentistry in the UK, maybe even Europe. Not bad for a boy born in Salford!

During this time, there has not been a single week when I have not been coaching dentists and their team, either in-house at their practice, or on one of my courses. I socialize more with dentists than I do my own wife and kids, so I feel I have earned the right to share what I consider are some common mistakes dentists and their teams make when communicating with patients.

Here they are, and they are in no particular order.

## Mistake Number One

One of the biggest mistakes dentists and orthodontists make is that they are too technical when talking to their patients. Every day you are immersed in dentistry and the vast majority of the courses you go on are technical, especially if you are a specialist. If you tell a patient that "an implant is a titanium screw that gets surgically screwed in your jaw bone under anaesthetic", then don't be too surprised if your patient loses interest. If you are an orthodontist and you tell your patient that you have "a bracket that is self-ligating, with low frictional forces and which uses heat activated niti wires containing 6% copper", then don't be surprised if they look confused.

Your patients do not live and breathe dentistry like you. If you talk this language to them, they are most likely going to switch off and be put off having treatment. On most occasions, patients do not actually care about the technical side of their treatment.

In 1937, Dale Carnegie wrote a book called "How to Win Friends and Influence People". One of the principles in the book is '**Try honestly to see things from the other person's point of view.**' In other words, take your shoes off and put your patient's shoes on and talk to them in their language, a language that they understand. Once you do this, then more patients will take on board your ideas.

## Mistake Number Two

One of the toughest things about sales, in fact one of the toughest things in life in general, is we often forget others don't necessarily share our passion about things.

So, for example, if you have an absolute burning passion for fishing and you live and breathe fishing every day, then it can often come to a shock when people do not share the same passion as you and actually could not care less.

This is the same for dentistry. You are treating patients for 4- 5 days a week, 44 weeks a year and then going on many courses learning the technical side of your profession, you are immersed in dentistry all your life. No-one, with the exception perhaps of other dentists, of course, cares anywhere near as much about your business, or your particular skill-set, the way you do.

So when you're out there trying to sell patients on something, you need to sell them results and solutions, not how good you are at delivering dentistry.

And it's sometimes hard to do this because you're so completely immersed in being the best at what you do -- it's hard to imagine anyone, especially your patients, not sharing, or appreciating, the pride of ownership you have, or how skilled you are and how competent your work is.

But rest assured, they don't appreciate it, because it's not their problem.

Patients will buy from you, because of the results you can deliver and nothing more. My clients do not care that I have delivered over 3,500 workshops and coached over 40,000 delegates in the last 18 years. They want to know the benefits and the results they will achieve by working with me. People buy results. A person does not buy a drill, he buys a hole. He buys what the drill will do for him.

When selling dentistry, sell results, solutions, and end benefits, and your patients will hear you loud and clear.

## Mistake Number Three

Imagine you were going to a restaurant and, as you walked to the front desk, there are two choices on where you can eat. You could eat in the bar and have a snack, or in the à la carte restaurant where you can have a five-course meal. The head waiter starts to look you up and down and, judging by the way you are dressed and look, offers you the bar snack menu.

How would you feel?

You might feel annoyed, insulted, and you might feel that you have been pre-judged and were not given the opportunity to decide for yourself where you wanted to eat. This is very similar to what some dentists do. One of the biggest mistakes dentists make is **trying to offer a solution to their patients, without first fully understanding their wants and needs.** In other words, they assume what they think the client requires.

I have had literally hundreds of dentists openly admit in my workshops that they have pre-judged a client when presenting treatment options. They have made assumptions by what the patient is wearing, what job they have, or even their postcode. When you do this, then you are nearly as bad as the head waiter. You will also miss out on opportunities.

Split the word assume up - ass u me. If you assume, you will make an ass out of you and me. Never make assumptions or pre-judge your patients, you will be missing out on many thousands of pounds worth of opportunities, and also the chance to deliver the dentistry that you spent many hours studying.

## Mistake Number Four

There are several elements to the sales process. These include building rapport, asking questions to find out what your patients requires, providing a solution and then talking money. So far you have already invested a lot of time and effort into the relationship. If you then hand a treatment plan to your patient and tell him/her to go away and think about it, that is probably exactly what they will do - think about it. All that time invested into the relationship may have been wasted. Mistake number four is not asking the patient if they want to proceed with the treatment, in other words not gaining commitment.

There are many reasons why dentists do not "close a sale". These include:

1. You don't like rejection
2. You don't want to sound pushy
3. It is un- comfortable
4. You were not taught these skills at Dental School
5. You don't know how to ask.

However, if you don't get the patient to commit, it doesn't matter how good your clinical skills are, you will never get a chance to use them. Even more upsetting is that your patients will never have the major benefits you can provide in their lives.

Take the 'c' out of close, you are left with lose. That's what happens when you don't close. You lose because you don't get to deliver the treatment and the patient loses because they do not receive the benefits your services can provide.

## Mistake Number Five

Imagine a scenario where you and your partner are having a disagreement over something trivial. Do you often find that a small disagreement can often escalate into a major row that lasts for hours, or even days?

Why does this happen?

I often find this happens because neither of the parties can see each other's point of view, in other words we get defensive about our own situation. The more defensive we become, the more defensive our partner becomes and that is why major rows can often break out.

One of the biggest mistakes dentists make is that when they get an objection from a patient they become all defensive and handle the objection badly, which then has a knock-on effect on the relationship between the dentist and the patient and thus the sale does not proceed.

When a patient raises an objection it is because he or she has not been convinced, is uncertain or has worries about the treatment. In other words, it has not been sold properly. Poor selling raises objections and you need to work on preventing objections rather than a cure. I often hear dentists reply to a price concern with comments such as:

- No, it is not expensive,
- What are you comparing it to
- It is not expensive, it is an investment
- Not really
- The price of the treatment is the same price as a short holiday.

When you use these statements, then you will only get your client's back up and they will think that you are not seeing things from their point of view and that you are not acting in their best interests. When this happens, the relationship can breakdown.

## Mistake Number Six
One of the mistakes I find dentists make is that they don't seem to invest the time into building the relationship with the patient. This might be a hangover from the NHS, where patients would walk in every 10 minutes. I once heard a dentist on one course tell me that "we put the patient on the chair and sometimes forget they have a heartbeat we are so busy looking at the clock on the wall to ensure that we are not running late."

## Mistake Number Seven
The good Lord gave us two ears and one mouth, but do we ever use them in this proportion? And that is another mistake I find dentists make, they listen to respond, rather than to understand.

Listen to respond is when you listen to the patient, but you are actually thinking what you are going to say back and what you are doing is waiting for a gap in the conversation to say your piece. If you are thinking what you are going to say back, it is impossible to really listen to your patients. You cannot do both at the same time.

Listen to understand is when you listen attentively to your patient, you are genuinely interested and you have no pre-conceived ideas. In other words, 100% of your whole focus is on the patient.

When you listen to respond, what happens? You make assumptions; offer the wrong solutions and invariably the relationship breaks down.

Can you relate to any of these mistakes?

The principles I am sharing with you are proven to work. I receive many testimonial letters and emails every week stating they have and I deliver over 20 of my Two Day Programmes every year. They must work, as I very rarely advertise and most of my business comes from clients repeating the programme or word of mouth.

I am sharing with you strategies and techniques that will help make your reception more effective, in other words, how to turn those opportunities into appointments. The rest of the book is dedicated to making it the best possible patient journey you can imagine. There are also some bonus material on how to follow up with your patients and also how to deal with any complaints they may have.

I have shared numerous examples and experiences, both my own and my clients', sometimes in a serious manner, but also in a light-hearted way. I am hoping you will be smiling one minute, then reading something that you need to do the next and even underlining some of the material as it relates to your situation.

## How to get the Best out of this Book
Knowledge is only power once you have used it and mastered it. So, please, as you read this book, here are some suggestions to help you get the best out of it.

1. Read each chapter twice, so the material sinks in better
2. Underline the material that is relevant and important, so that you can refer back to it at a later date.
3. At the end of each chapter, read the Things to do section and take action
4. Ensure that your whole team reads this book. Better still, buy them a copy of this book and read it together and then you can discuss the principles in team meetings.

I am biased, but I believe the information in this book is vital and it will give you the edge.

Enjoy the journey.

Chapter One:

# Making a Superb First Impression on the Telephone

In 1994 I visited San Diego for a Dale Carnegie World Conference. Not only was this my first conference, but my first visit to America and I was like a kid in a sweet shop. I was so excited.

On the second night I was taken to a restaurant chain called Ruth Chris, famous for their steaks. I remember walking into that restaurant as if it were only yesterday and being met by two greeters who had the most amazing welcome and smile. They escorted my party to a table near the bar, where we were greeted by a further two waiters, who gave us all menus. One waiter then asked us if we would like a drink and we all proceeded to give him our drinks order. I was surprised that he didn't write any of this down, bearing in mind that there were 13 in my party. The waiter came back literally 10 minutes later and gave us all our drinks in perfect order. I was so impressed. He then gave us a short presentation on the specials that they had that evening. We had only been in the restaurant for 15 minutes and I was literally blown away with the excellent customer service and the superb first impression they had made.

What's more, the meal was excellent and we visited the restaurant on a further three more occasions during our one week stay. On each occasion the service and food were equally as good. You can imagine on our last night, the waiters were all our best friends. There were two other incidents that also stood out on my visits to Ruth Chris. The staff there would not allow us to take photographs. They took them all for us on the basis that it was better that we were all in the pictures. On one occasion the batteries in my camera ran out and they sent one of their staff to go to buy me batteries, so that I could take photos that night. How good was that?

I have told this story umpteen times on my travels all over the UK and I have recommended many friends to eat at a Ruth Chris restaurant when they have visited the States. They have all come back with similar world class customer service tales.

Let's look at the other side of making a first impression.

My parents, who now live in St. Annes near Blackpool, were having a party on a Sunday afternoon a few months ago. My brother rang me and suggested that it would be a good idea if the two families stayed in a hotel the night before and had a family get together. My brother has, like me two children and when we get together, the cousins play really well together. I thought it was a great idea and said I would contact the hotel that we have both stayed in on several occasions. It is a family hotel, with a swimming pool, play area and the food is great. Our children love the hotel and it is real treat for them.

Here is how the conversation went, more or less word for word: (I am AL and the receptionist is SPO – the "Sales Prevention Officer")

AL: Hello, can I please book two family rooms for a week on Saturday-do you have availability? (By the way I am holding my credit card in my hand)

SPO: Yes, we have availability, but I cannot offer you those rooms, unless you stay Friday night as well.

AL: I am sorry, but my brother works on a Saturday and we can only stay on the Saturday, can you please accommodate us?

SPO: No, I am sorry, it is the policy of the hotel.

AL: We really like your hotel; do you have any family rooms available?

SPO: Yes, they are all available.

AL: How much is it to stay then?

SPO: £165 a night, bed and breakfast

AL: So, for two nights it would be that times two?

SPO: Yes.

AL: There is no way you can accommodate us then?

SPO: No, I am sorry.

AL: Right, so it looks like you cannot help me here?

SPO: I am afraid not, sorry.

AL: Bye then.

SPO: Good night.

Firstly, let me please acknowledge one thing, I respect their business model. If they fill their rooms just for one night then it is obviously going to affect their profits, as they would be turning away weekend bookings. I understand, I am in business myself. I would not let my clients just come for one day on my two-day course as it would not benefit anyone. Secondly, I don't want to appear to be bashing the British hotel industry, as I have had some wonderful experiences in my time.

However, there were several things that this receptionist could have done:

1.  Asked me my name and thanked me for enquiring about their services. This is very easy if she uses her name when she answers the telephone. She could have said my name is Jane and your name is? She could have then used it in the conversation and built excellent rapport with me.
2.  She should have definitely asked us how we had heard about the hotel. This is essential in marketing as the hotel is probably spending thousands of pounds advertising in magazines, newspapers, even with a Google ad campaign.

The hotel needs to know if they are spending their money wisely and getting a return on their investment.

3. If the receptionist had taken my name and checked her computer, she would have established that we had stayed at the hotel several times before and were existing, happy customers. There is nothing like repeat business, it is free, price is not normally an issue and you don't get any objections – perfect! The whole relationship and conversation could have been so different.

4. She could have been flexible and, on this occasion, offered us the rooms. She did say that they were all available. This was November in Blackpool; probably a quiet time for the hotel industry and, after all, it was less than ten days before we were to visit the hotel. They should have an idea if they were likely to sell those rooms or not.

5. She could have spoken to the Manager and asked if they could change the rules on this occasion, as we were regular customers.

6. At the very least, she could have taken my details and offered to ring back in a few days time, if they had not sold any weekend packages and offer us the rooms.

I would have been delighted if the hotel had given us the last option, as our family likes the hotel, our children love this hotel and are used to the surroundings and the facilities. If you are a parent you will know that if your kids are happy, so are you.

The result was no sale and a lost opportunity. The hotel probably lost a sale of around £600, after all we would have had dinner there, plus a few bottles of wine etc. They have probably lost future sales from us as well.

This incident really brought home to me how important the receptionist area is in your practice. He/she can make or break your practice. A good receptionist is worth their weight in gold. A bad one has the potential to ruin your practice.

If anyone has watched "Little Britain" you will be familiar with the scene in the travel shop where the agent says those words to her customers: "The computer says no."

It really does happen out there!

There is a saying:

**You never get a second chance to make a first impression.**

Here is another story to back up the importance of first impressions. Four years ago a brand new gym opened up a mile down the road from where we live. My wife was very keen to join the gym and asked me to see what it was like and to get some membership details. I already belonged to a gym in Manchester and I was not as enthusiastic as her, however I visited the gym on a Monday morning as requested.

I entered the reception where there were three receptionists at the desk. I asked if I could please be shown around the gym as I was interested in joining. One of the girls stated that they were not allowed to show me around and I would have to come back at 10am when the sales people arrived. I stated that I could not come back at 10am as I was going to work, but was it possible one of the three could show me around. Again they stated they were not allowed, it was the rules of the gymnasium and that I had to come back at 10am. Not being put off, I persisted. Yes, I am the one now persisting, and I asked again if it was possible that I could very quickly look at the gym, which was up a flight of stairs. Again they stated no, but they did give me a list of all the classes. On this occasion, the rules of the gymnasium got in the way and, with no flexibility at all, this was a lost opportunity for the gym.

I actually went back at 10.10am to be shown around the gym and, later in the book; I will carry on with this story.

Before I share some more tips on how to answer the telephone and make a brilliant first impression, here is a question that needs answering?

## What is the lifetime value of an average patient to your practice?
Why is this important, let's see?

Say, for example, a patient is on a membership scheme with you and they pay £17 per month. For the purpose of this discussion, they stay with you for 20 years. That means, without the patient even spending a penny on treatment with you, which I am sure they will, conservatively allowing for inflation and membership increases, this patient could possibly spend £5,000-£6,000 over a lifetime with you. This also does not include any referrals they may give you, such as family members or friends, or any treatments, so this figure could easily be double or even treble this amount.

So, why is this important? I want your receptionist and everyone in the practice to answer the telephone as if this patient is worth £7,000 to the practice.

If they did, would they possibly handle the phone calls differently than they do now?

In your next team meeting, have a discussion and ask this question: what is the lifetime value of a patient to the practice? It is certainly worth a discussion.

Each new lead for your practice should be treated like gold dust. I know that's what we do in our business. We know through experience, that each client is worth many thousands of pounds. We have clients who have taken several programmes with us and they have also introduced many new clients to our business. Our business depends on word-of-mouth.

Another thing that you also need to consider is this. I honestly believe that if patients are calling your practice enquiring about your services, they are genuinely interested in buying your services. Let's say for example, you have an adult patient enquiring about orthodontic treatment and they contact your practice. The chances are the patient has been thinking about having this treatment done for many months, even years. During this period, they could have read articles, seen someone else have the treatment and seen themselves on a video and not liked what they saw. They might have then done some research on the internet and then finally picked up the telephone to make an appointment with you. If they are doing this, then they are genuinely ready to move to the next stage. I know you do get some tyre kickers (people who waste time), but on the whole, I believe if patients are contacting you, they are ready to move to the next stage. People do not generally create a list of people to call just to annoy them and waste their time. So treat the call like gold dust. Each phone call is potentially worth thousands of pounds to you and your practice. Make sure it is your practice they choose and not someone else's.

Another exercise I urge you to do to is to get your receptionist to ask further questions and dig for more information. Perhaps the patient saw your website and it prompted them to contact you; ask the patient what it was about your website that he or she liked. Again it is useful information, especially if you are constantly updating your website, as you can establish what your potential clients like about the current format. If it is a referral, find out who the introducer was and you can then thank them in an appropriate way. This is vital information to your practice. If it is a referral, it will be easy to build a rapport with the new patient and it will also demonstrate that you already have a happy client.

At a further team meeting, I urge you to ask this question and discuss it in detail. What are some of the things that frustrate you when you ring up a company? You can then look at what you do in your practice and see what you feel might frustrate your clients when they contact you. For example, do you have a rule that the telephone should be answered in a certain number of rings? I think ideally it should be answered in four rings. If you do this exercise, please make sure that you are not in any way criticising the reception team, but you are just looking at ways to improve customer service.

## The role of the receptionist

So what is the role of the receptionist? This is my personal view:

1. To build rapport with the patient/make a friend
2. To find out what the patient's issues/problems are
3. To solve the patient's immediate problems by making an appointment

As I have already stated, the receptionist can build rapport by asking the patient's name, asking them how they heard about the practice, and then asking further questions to find out a little bit more information on what in particular the patient is interested in. Let's say a patient is interested in orthodontic treatment, then the receptionist can ask a few questions such as:

How can we help you?

You mentioned invisible braces, what is it about them that interest you?

What is it about having straighter teeth that is particularly important for you?

All the receptionist is doing here is becoming genuinely interested. The answers they receive will determine the next question.

Once you have done this, then you can go onto stage three which is inviting the patient in for an appointment. An example on how to ask for an appointment is:

Mrs Patient, when would be a suitable time and date for you to visit us, so that Dr. Jones can give you an examination and explore in more detail what your goals are and your options are?

If I am coaching in dental practices, I always say to the receptionists, to use the KISS script, "KEEP IT SIMPLE STUPID". I would not advise the receptionists to talk too much about the treatment that is the role of the dentist. If you can also avoid talking about prices, that might also be a benefit. If the patient wants some idea on price, then you can give your potential client the range of prices as a guide. Always go back to telling the patient, that, once they come into the practice, then the dentist can find out exactly what the issues are. Remember the receptionist's goal is to make an appointment.

If there is a fee for the appointment, try to build the value of the appointment. For example, I often hear the receptionist say: "The fee is £ 200." Instead, why don't you say something like this?

"Your comprehensive treatment assessment with Dr. Jones is £197. This includes a full assessment which involves impressions, x-rays, photos and your full treatment plan, which explains detailed options, and a second visit, if needed. If you do decide to go ahead with the treatment, then we will knock this initial fee off your treatment plan.

Mrs Smith, does this sound okay? Is a morning or afternoon appointment better for you?"

In other words, always let the patient know what they are getting for their money.

If the patient is put off by paying a fee beforehand, then you could offer a 20-minute discussion with a Treatment Co-ordinator or Practice Manager where again further options can be discussed and you can give the client a tour of the practice. Then if they are happy, hopefully you can move to the next step.

If the reception staff follows the above steps, then I don't think you can go far wrong.

Wherever possible, your receptionist should ask further questions and dig for more information, for example, about how the potential patient found you and, if from your website or a referral, try and get details.

As you read this, I know what you are saying. This all sounds great, but in an ideal world, the reception team is busy and they are dealing with patients at the desk. They won't have time to do all this.

There is a simple solution, this is going to be revolutionary and will certainly get you thinking. For the dentists who have done this, it has made a massive difference to their results and customer service. The next sentence may surprise you, so be prepared.

Take the telephone out of reception. Yes, take the telephone out of reception.

It is impossible to do an outstanding job on the telephone and, at the same time, deal with your patients in reception. If you spend a long time with people on the telephone, then you will annoy the patients in reception. If you treat your telephone enquiries like hot potatoes, in other words, you are rushing to get them off the telephone, then, with the best will in the world, you will miss opportunities.

You can set up another room in the practice and call it the Business Room, or something similar. Here you can have the telephoned manned full time and the people who work in this room can get on with other important jobs within the practice. The single major advantage of doing this is that the telephone calls will get 100% of the reception team's attention. The calls will get dealt with superbly well and the patients will be delighted to receive undivided attention. When I deliver my programme, I ask the reception team how many new telephone calls they receive and they often tell me from 5 to 10 a week. It won't take too long before removing the phone from reception will really make a difference to your income. Don't forget an average patient life time value is £7,000.

I know this might be difficult if a practice has not got the room. You might even consider creating this room out of the practice. It is only a thought; after all with technology nowadays, you can work anywhere. My PA works from home and is never in my office.

## Answer Machines

For many years I have been preaching about the negative impact an answer machine can have in your practice and I want to expand on it a little bit more here.

Around ten years ago, I was delivering an in-house course in Doncaster. I was actually running the programme in the large reception area of the practice. As the course was for the whole practice, they put the answer machine on for the whole day. On the first morning we were having a break and whilst we were having a coffee, the receptionist checked the messages. On the telephone machine, it stated that the telephone had rung 29 times, but interestingly only 8 patients had left messages. 21 people rang the practice up and on hearing the answer machine, had put the telephone down. I started questioning the receptionist and I discovered that the answer machine was always on at lunch time and over the next 2 days that I was there, we discovered that the practice had received 22 calls and only 5 had left messages. I was obviously shocked to hear these statistics.

If a patient wants to undertake some personal business, the time they will probably do it will be over lunch time. If you are closed and you leave an answer machine on then there is a strong likelihood that the caller will not leave a message. There also is a strong possibility that these people could be new patients wanting to book appointments and enquire about your services. If on average 10 people rang everyday at lunch time, over 50 weeks, there are a lot of calls going straight to a machine and no messages being left.

In fairness, this was a busy mixed practice and you might not get the same number of calls. Do you have an answer machine on in your practice? If you do, then you could be missing out on many thousands of pounds worth of new opportunities, on the basis that each new patient is potentially worth £7,000 to you over a lifetime.

I am writing this book during the deepest, longest recession the country has had for many years and I am just not sure that answer machines have a role in the 21st Century Dental Practice. Today, I contacted a practice in Scotland and, without a word of a lie, the message said that the practice was closed between 1pm and 2pm and that I should ring back after lunch. There wasn't even a space where I could leave a message, it was as blunt as that. Why don't you play your message back and put your patient's shoes on and listen to the message. It is amazing how quickly the person speaks as they try and leave a one-minute message in a 30-second space. I often find it is impossible to write down the emergency telephone number, even when I have a pen and paper in my hand.

The excuses I often hear for having an answer machine is that the reception team like to have their lunch together and it is good team bonding. However, can you imagine going to a retail shop and there are no staff on the floor because they are all having lunch together? It just wouldn't happen. Patients want to look ten years younger and there is a lot more interest in having their teeth looking great and having a nice smile. If you offer these services, then you must stay open all day and allow your potential clients to speak with you. If you don't, the patient will not leave a message but will ring another practice where they can speak to a human being.

If you have a small team and you believe it would be very difficult for the telephone to be answered all the time, then another solution is to get the telephone answered by an outside company. There are a number of these companies and they will answer the telephone on your behalf, using your name and then they will take a message. Within a few minutes that message can be either texted or emailed to your practice and then a member of your team can ring the clients back and deal with their enquiry. The patients will be delighted as the telephone has been answered and, as far as they're concerned, they have spoken with your practice direct. This is a good solution to the answer machine, at the very least your clients are getting some good human contact. Of the various companies that offer this service, I recommend a company called Answer4you, their website is www.answer-4u.com/. Mention my name and there is a special programme available. As I am writing this book, I am using their services and am a satisfied customer. I know a few clients who use this service and the feedback has also been very positive. The other major advantage of using this type of service is that you can have the telephone answered to suit you. For example, Nadim Majid runs a dental practice from Blackburn and spends quite a lot of his time and investment on search engine optimization and ad-words. If you go to his excellent website, **www.lifestyledental. co.uk**, you will see that he operates a 7-day 24-hour service. The calls after 5pm are answered by a telephone answering company and he can capture all the enquiries by a human being. Nadim does not leave it to chance whether the patient will leave a message with an answering machine or not. He has been amazed how many people will do their research at night time and then ring the practice there and then. He reckons that he gets around 25 calls a month after 5pm. In the space of 2 years he has built a very successful practice from a squat.

## Turning NHS Enquiries into Patients

I was delivering one of my two-day in-house courses a few years ago in Derbyshire. The aim of the course was to help improve private treatment, but also help the reception team promote and sell the maintenance plan the practice had in place - I believe it was Denplan.

Over the two days I was observing how the team worked and, in particular, the reception team. I noticed that on a few occasions patients were contacting the practice enquiring about NHS treatment and the reception team were stating that they did not offer this service and ending the call. Partly because I am nosy, but also because I am always looking at opportunities, I asked one of the girls how many calls they received like this in a day or week. I was shocked to hear that they received something like five calls a day over 50 weeks, which of course adds up to over 1,250 patients asking about NHS services. We had some further discussion and I coached the team on the telephone. Before we knew it we had developed a script for those clients making these enquiries on the telephone.

In short, when a patient asked if the practice did NHS work, they stated that they didn't but asked the patient if they had a problem at this moment. They went on to say that they were a private practice and offered this type of treatment for as little as £12 per month. They then asked if they would like to visit to view the practice and see if it fitted their needs. As a result, one in three patients said yes.

You see there are opportunities everywhere. I believe that most patients believe that private treatment is very expensive and don't realise, that for a few pounds per month, they could have first class private treatment. Can you see how important your reception team are? Before the training they were turning over 1,250 patients away, without informing them what the practice can do, and now they have an extra 400 patients a year, worth an extra £4,000 per month, and that is before they have had any treatment. I reckon they had a good return from my programme.

Another great way of making a superb first impression on the telephone is to have a system whereby you know the name of the person who is calling you. I know that there are a number of companies that offer this software. You key in your clients' telephone numbers and, when they ring your practice, you see their name coming up on a screen. You can then answer your telephone stating your own name, name of the practice and greet your patients by their own name. (Software of Excellence www.softwareofexcellence.co.uk offers this system).

As you have read, a good reception team can make or break your practice. It can add thousands of extra pounds to your turnover and can also lose you thousands of pounds of lost opportunities. That is why, in 2010, I started to deliver my one day **Reception Programmes**, which is all about turning enquiries into appointments. For more information on this subject, please visit my website www.ashleylatter.com and click onto the Reception Programme.

As the receptionist is often the first person the patient will see at the practice, she can also create a wonderful, re-assuring experience. I want to end this chapter with a personal story which sums up their importance.

Around the start of 2010, I was experiencing a horrendous chest infection which seemed to last for many weeks. I had two courses of antibiotics with no effect at all. If truth be known, I should have had a week in bed, but I carried on working. Anyway, one night I was feeling quite poorly and I had a trip down to London the next morning to deliver a two-day course. My chest started to feel very tight. It was about 5pm and, as I had had pneumonia in the past, my wife suggested that I should go to the accident and emergencies centre at Bury General Hospital, our local hospital. My first response was no, as my impression was that it will would only deal with emergencies, however, my wife put me in the car and told me to go. I must confess driving to the hospital I was thinking the worst and I had visions of being turned away and told to go to a doctor. However nothing could be further from the truth. When I told the receptionist how I was feeling, she came round from the other side of her desk and re-assured me that I was in the right place. She promised I would get my chest x-rayed that night and told me that I had done the right thing. Within ten minutes I saw a nurse, who obviously had heard the story from the receptionist and again re-assured me that I was in the right place (baton getting past on) and within two hours I had my chest x-rayed, prescriptions and tablets in my pocket and a good bye that was as good as my first greeting. I could not fault them. The customer service and sincerity from every member of staff was world class.

## Things to do

1. Have a discussion with your team and write down all the things that annoy you when you ring up businesses and document what they say
2. Have a discussion about when you had a great experience and again document the findings
3. Based on this, have a look at your practice and see if there is anything that can be improved and changed
4. Develop and coach your reception team, and develop scripts if necessary, on how to answer the telephone
5. Coach and practice these scripts until your team can say them off by heart. The last thing you want is your team to be reading scripts, as they won't listen properly
6. Finally measure, measure, measure everything

## Chapter Two:
# **Building Rapport**

I am going to go through the most important skill that you can possess. In fact if you have this skill in your make up, you will be welcome anywhere in the world. The key skill here is the ability to build rapport with people. If you can build rapport with your clients, colleagues and suppliers, then people are more likely to listen to you, take on board your suggestions and, most importantly, trust you. Without rapport, then the rest of the sales process will just not happen. I have learned over thousands of appointments and interactions in my life that people always buy people first, before anything else. Have you ever tried to buy anything off anyone you don't like or trust? It's not easy.

All our successes in life, and you will have your own definition of success, are created by interaction with other people. We cannot persuade people if you have little or no rapport with them.

My definition of rapport building is when you have a mutual understanding and trust. You are on the same wavelength, in-sync with the person you are speaking to. Let me share with you a personal story that happened to me a few years ago which backs up the importance of building rapport.

I decided to finance a friend of mine who is a builder, to buy a very run down property in the Bury area of Manchester, with a view to renovating the property and then selling it once the work had finished.

The property was in a good area and I was very confident that we could make a profit on the deal, and it fitted with my risk taking. However I needed to borrow £150,000 very quickly. I believed I had sufficient equity in my house and that I would not have a problem borrowing the money. So, I contacted my existing bank, for the purpose of this story let's call them EXISTING BANK. I had been a customer with this bank for over 19 years and I had two accounts with them. To ensure that I was getting a really good deal, I also contacted a client banker who I did some training with, for the purpose of this story, let's call them NEW BANK. I asked EXISTING BANK to visit my house at 2pm and NEW BANK at 4pm.

EXISTING BANK arrived. Two ladies who were pleasant and we built up some positive rapport. However, I was gob-smacked when one of them asked me what I did for a living. I would have thought after 20 years as a customer they would know this information. To be honest, once I started explaining what I did to my existing bankers of 20 years, I got frustrated and a little annoyed. I didn't feel important and I more or less decided there and then that I was not going to use their services.

Brian Hargreaves from NEW BANK arrived on time and then he started asking me questions about my business in particular about the work that I did with dentists, which he'd discovered after his research visiting my website. He also complimented me on my website and the articles that appeared on it. We must have spent at least 20 minutes discussing my business and my life and I was in my element. You see ME is my favourite conversation! Brian asked questions about what I required and presented some quotations that he had already prepared on the basis of a quick conversation we had on the telephone the day before. There was an instant rapport and an excellent relationship had been established. I decided there and then that I was going to do work with Brian. I felt comfortable with Brian and a real trust had been established. In fact, I handed over the deeds to my house to Brian, a person I had never met before, within 30 minutes of meeting him, rather than to two ladies from the bank where I had been a customer for 20 years. That's what happens when you build rapport with people. People always buy people first.

Let's analyse a few things that Brian did and a few lessons that you can take away to build instant rapport with your patients:

1. He did his preparation. He visited my website and learned about me before he came to see me. Do you always review your patients' notes before your patients come and see you? You can review their past history, or the notes that you made last time about something personal. This will enable you to build excellent rapport with your patient. If it is a new patient, please speak with your reception team or treatment co-ordinator and see what they have learnt about the patient and that way you can again build that instant rapport. I recently spoke with Ashish Parmar, a dentist from Hertford who was on Extreme Makeover, and he insists that,

before he sees a new patient, he knows at least five facts about them.

2. He told me that he thought my website was great and was full of interesting articles and stories. He paid me a compliment and did it sincerely. If you ever compliment another person it is a great way of building rapport, but you must be sincere.

3. He was genuinely interested in me as a person and got me to do most of the talking. Because of his interest in me, I became interested in him. He got me talking about my favourite subject, which is me. What is your favourite subject?

4. He asked good questions to find out exactly what I was looking for and he was therefore able to offer me the correct solution to my needs. The next chapter is devoted to this topic alone.

5. He was an excellent listener and he truly listened to what I wanted and the urgency needed to finance the house purchase.

6. He took the time to get to know me as a person before we went into the business side of the meeting. I remember a dentist friend called Tim Thackarah telling me once that sometimes we forget that our patients have heartbeats. Sometimes we are more interested in looking at the clock, to see if we are running to time.

As a side issue, Brian also noticed various pictures of Manchester United on my walls and, as he is also a supporter, we very quickly struck up a conversation about our common interests. This obviously helped our relationship together. Have you ever met a stranger, struck up a conversation and all of a sudden you find you have a common interest? Before you know it you have been speaking for ages and, sudden, you find you have developed a really strong relationship.

This guy had "Ashley Lattered" me!

Let me also explain what happened over the next few days.

1. One of Brian's associates came and collected the forms within 12 hours of our meeting, personally at my house.
2. I had regular telephone calls from his PA Stephanie informing me of the progress of the loan
3. Once we had completed, I got a telephone call telling me the money was ready and available to spend
4. A few days later I got a bunch of flowers thanking me for my business and for choosing NEW BANK.

It was harder to do business with NEW BANK as I had to provide them with the information that my existing bank already had. There were more forms to complete, however it was a joy to do business with them.

A few years later, I now have my business account, the mortgage on my house, my public liability insurance and other related products and services all with Brian Hargreaves, and I have regular meetings with Brian. This is all business that my first bank has lost as they did not know what I did for a living and hence could not build rapport with me. It seems crazy thinking about it that representatives from my old bank visited me and did not know what I did.

I find in life that for every 100 purchases/transactions I make about 3-4% are memorable and enjoyable. The other 96% are okay, nothing special, or the service etc is not good and you don't enjoy it. So I am delighted to share one of the 3-4% experiences.

So, before a patient visits your practice, spend some time reading their notes beforehand. They might have told you about a treatment they wanted last time. If so, then perhaps you can get some of your evidence ready to show just in case it crops up again in conversation. Maybe last time they mentioned something important going on in their lives and you can read up on it before the patient comes in. You can then bring it up in conversation and your patient will be delighted that you remembered.

If you have a new patient visiting your practice, then you can have a meeting with the receptionists or the treatment co-ordinator, if you have one, and ask them for some background information. If you're like the dentist Ashish Parmar, you'll look for five interesting facts about the patient before seeing them, so that you have the best possible chance to build rapport with them. It makes the patient feel important and shows that you care.

I always suggest, if you can, to find two chairs, or maybe construct a consulting room, and to have a conversation with your patient before you put them on the dental chair. It might be a scary experience for a patient to go to the dentist and having a two-way conversation puts the patient at ease and makes them feel important. If you have not got two chairs and your surgery space does not allow it, then perhaps you can put the patient on the dental chair in an upright position and you can bring your chair round facing the patient. It shows that you are genuinely interested and, most importantly, it will put the client at ease.

I am going to slightly contradict myself here and say that you only build rapport with friendly people. You are sometimes going to get a stern or serious patient who will not want to do rapport building. If this is the case, then you need to be serious and stern as well. In other words, you are probably best being business-like and mirroring your patient. Why? Because if you try and be friendly with unfriendly people, they will probably go the other way. In any case, it is virtually impossible to do this. You have probably got many experiences of this in your lifetime. In a future chapter of this book, I go into personality styles in more detail.

Here is my quick checklist to build rapport with your clients:

1. Smile - please make sure you do this sincerely and also that your teeth look the part. This also goes for all the team members of the practice. You need to walk the talk. As a side issue, I know Practices who have told me that their teeth whitening procedures/sales have increased, once the whole team had their own teeth whitened.

2. Become genuinely interested in your patient, and then they will become genuinely interested in what you have to offer. Patients don't care

> what you know, until you first demonstrate that you care about them.

3. Make the patient feel important. It's show time! Treat the appointment like an event, make it special.
4. Pay your patient a compliment, and do it sincerely
5. Do your preparation beforehand, read the notes and have a team huddle about the patients coming in that day
6. Relax and be yourself. Don't try and be something that you are not.
7. Use their name in the conversation and ensure that you are pronouncing it correctly if it is an unusual name. Don't be afraid, by the way, to ask to get it right. Patients will be impressed that you took an interest.

I am not on any royalty payments or inducements (I just happened to work for the organisation for 10 years!), but I urge you to read Dale Carnegie's **"How to Win friends and Influence People"**. It was first published in 1937 and it does exactly what it says on the tin. You will discover 36 human relation principles that you can use in your everyday life that will help you build relationships and win people to your way of thinking. It is more relevant today, then when it was first written. Please also ensure that your whole team read the book and, in your team meetings, share the principles and how you have used them. I promise your practice will be a better place when your team reads this book.

As I mentioned in the previous chapter, over a lifetime, a single patient is worth thousands of pounds to your practice and this relationship needs to be nourished on an ongoing basis. I have learnt in my lifetime, never to take my clients for granted, whenever I have, it has come back to bite me in the backside. If you have excellent relationships with your clients, then you are more likely to get referrals from them. I usually find that if some of these patients are nice and value what you do, then you are more likely to get people of similar characteristics. Nice people know nice people.

I doubt by reading this chapter that you have learnt anything new or anything that I have written has been a revelation to you. All this stuff is common sense, the problem with common sense is that it sometimes is not very common.

After my course, a practice decided to collect their patients from the reception and take them to the surgery and then escort them back to the desk after each appointment. They even got the reception team to ring through to the nurse to inform her what the patient was wearing, so that when she went to collect the patient, the nurse could go straight to the patient and use their name. That really is going the extra mile.

Talking about going the extra mile, a few years ago, I took Grace to see Billy Elliott at the Theatre in London. I must confess I am not a great Theatre goer, I can often get bored and fidgety. However, I enjoyed the film and I was looking forward to seeing the show live.

The show was not only superb, but great fun and entertaining and at the end of the show there was a standing ovation that lasted for several minutes. I turned round to one of the staff members and suggested that we were lucky tonight, as we had seen the best performance of this show ever. She politely disagreed with me and told me that it was like this every night and that is why it was all the performances were sold out. After further discussion, she went onto inform me that the next time you could get a ticket was in a few months time.

The conversation left me invigorated. Here was a show that the cast do every day, the same words and actions and yet they perform like it was day one. You feel that after some performances you might feel that they would find it hard to get motivated. Yet every day it is a different audience that sees the show and that is why I suspect that they get all this motivation. Is it show time every day in your surgery? Don't forget some of your patients have never seen the act before. This statement had a profound effect on me and I always think of Billy Elliott before I present my courses.

Before I leave this chapter, I want to share another story with you that sums up the value of applying these principles, especially when you go the extra mile in building relationships.

I was delivering one of my courses in Northern Ireland and I got asked by a dentist how should he deal with email enquiries. I told him how to write a reply, but then I suggested that he should ring the client up and build rapport and ask further questions on their wants and needs. This he did and he managed to speak to a patient who was interested in having three implants to replace some old dentures. She was in her late 60's and she also lived in the Republic and had found the dentist on the internet. The dentist offered her a free consultation and when he found out the patient was travelling by train, offered to pick her up from the station and bring her to the practice and take her back again.

The dentist spent a long time building rapport with the patient, to understand her wants and needs and eventually the patient decided to go ahead with the treatment, even though it meant a day's travelling.

On each visit, the patient was duly picked up at the station and taken back. On her final visit, she told the whole team how overwhelmed she was with the treatment and final results. She also went onto say that she never experienced customer service like it in her life. She even gave the whole team a £250 tip for all their trouble, and, of course, she introduced several friends and relatives to the practice.

I reckon 98% of practices would have probably contacted the patient by email and then never heard from the patient again and an opportunity would have gone somewhere else. Nothing beats a good conversation. Don't you find it frustrating when you ring your utility company, bank or mobile phone company that it is such hard work to get to speak to a person; you have to press 75 buttons beforehand. A lot of business is done on the internet and, with everyone wearing IPods in their ears, there is less communication than ever before. If you can go the other way and have this passion for building relationships and rapport, you will stand out from the crowd, no matter how crowded it is.

To conclude this chapter, I would like to share one of my favourite rapport building stories that truly states how important this part of the Ethical Sales approach is and a story with many lessons to take away.

One of my clients is a dentist called Simon Belford, who has a Practice in the South of England. He took my Ethical Sales & Communication Programme in the early part of 2014 and subsequently has taken it on a further two occasions. He is of the opinion that the more you practice and personalise these skills, the more comfortable you become communicating with your patients and more patients will take up treatment with someone who is genuinely interested in them as a person as well as their presenting issues.

He received an enquiry from a potential patient one evening, who was asking about Implant Treatment. Simon responded back to the patient more or less straight away. When we have discussed this on my courses, some of my delegates have stated that it sounded like a state of desperation, but I thought in this day and age the fact that Simon responded immediately, was pretty impressive.

The patient responded back the next day and subsequently an appointment was made for the following week. The night before his new appointment, Simon did his research about the patient by going on line and he soon discovered his patient was a Professional Speaker and had many videos on You Tube, which Simon subsequently watched.

The next morning after a morning huddle with the rest of his team, Simon welcomed the patient, where he built instant rapport with him, asked questions about his job as a speaker and a genuine rapport was built between the two of them. After questioning the patient about his problem and after a thorough examination took place, a large treatment plan was agreed between Simon and the patient and most importantly, a new relationship was formed. The natural conclusion was a win -win for both parties.

The lessons you can take away from this story are;

1. If you receive a new enquiry, act quickly, speed is important. We live in an age of instant communication and I honestly believe people are becoming more impatient, so act straight away.

2. There is no excuse now not to do your preparation. Years ago, there was only the local library for resources, now there are many such as going on line, do a Google search and try Facebook and LinkedIn. You can learn so much about a new person in seconds, by the push of a button.

3. I am a massive fan of group huddles in the morning before the patients walk through the door. Sometimes, if the Receptionist has done a good job at the initial call, then they can share with the rest of the team important information about the new patients who are coming into the Practice that day.

4. By spending time building genuine rapport, trust was built. Without trust, there is no rapport, without rapport, no transaction can take place.

I hope after reading this chapter you look at how you can take your relationships to a different level. Once you do this, new opportunities will be created that produce results better than your wildest dreams for you and your team.

## Things to do

1. Treat every appointment like an event - make it special for each patient
2. Remember to prepare for each appointment, if necessary have a group huddle
3. Ensure that your team follow the Human Relation Principles discussed in this book
4. Remember it is show time. We are all in show business, because we are constantly on show from first thing in the morning to last thing at night.

In the next chapter, I have written about the biggest mistakes dentists make in the selling process and also the value of asking further questions to your patients. If you can master these skills, you will create more opportunities than you can cope with.

Chapter Three:
# Asking Questions

"I keep six honest serving-men

(They taught me all I knew);

Their names are What and Why and When

And How and Where and Who."

**Rudyard Kipling**

So far in the process we have made an excellent first impression, we have built rapport with our clients, the next step in the process is to ask questions to find out if our patients have any problems, or issues that they would like addressed.

There are many advantages to asking our patients questions. These include:

1. Your patients will tell you what is bothering them, or if they have any issues that they want addressing. They will tell you their problems
2. It might create opportunities for you
3. You are still building rapport with your clients, so it makes your relationship stronger
4. You will be able to make recommendations that are on the patient's agenda and not yours

5. The main advantage is that it will stop you making assumptions, as I explained earlier in the book. The biggest mistake dentists and orthodontists make is that they make assumptions and try offering a solution to a patient without first finding out what the patient's wants and needs are. Let me repeat this because, if you get nothing else from this book but take this concept away with you, then you will have better and stronger relationships with your patients and you will create more opportunities. It is so important that I have dedicated several pages to this topic later in the chapter.

Let's look at the other side of the table: What does the patient get from the experience? They will be happy and they will feel important as someone is genuinely interested in them. Where do you go where someone sits down with you and shows that they genuinely care and are interested in them and their issues?

So, there are many advantages to both parties when we ask the patient questions about their wants and needs.

## Two Types of Questions

When you are asking questions there are two types of questions: open and closed.

When you ask a closed question you can only get a yes or no answer.

For example:

Are you happy with your appearance at the moment?

Have you any problems or issues?

As you can only get a yes or no answer, it will not be a very long conversation.

The other type of question you need to ask are open questions. These are questions where you get the patient to elaborate in more detail, so that you get a longer answer. Examples of these are:

Mrs Jones, what do you think about the current state of your teeth?

Mrs Jones, if we had a magic wand, how would you like your smile to look at the end of treatment?

When we are asking questions, please ensure that you ask a mixture of both, but mainly open questions or you are going to have a very short conversation.

So let's look at the questioning structure we can use in the consultation. There is a structure of four types of questions. These include **current** situation questions, **desired** situation questions**, implication** type of questions and **what's-in-it-for-me** questions.

Let's start off with **current** situation questions. These are questions we ask the patient so we can fully understand what their position is now.

Examples of these questions are:

Have you any problems at the moment?

If there was anything that you would like to change about your smile, what would it be?

On a scale of 1-10, how would you rate your smile at present? 1 you are not happy, 10 you are delighted.

If the patient is a new patient here are some must-ask questions:

How did you hear about our practice?

When was the last time you visited the dentist?

Which practice did you go to?

Do you mind me asking what made you change?

Here are some good questions to ask your patient if you are an orthodontist:

Mr Patient, have you considered how you would like to straighten your teeth?

Have you done any research on this, if so what is important to you?

How long have you been thinking about having the treatment?

These questions are very important because if you are spending money on marketing or advertising, such as

Google Ads etc, then you need to know if you are getting a return on your investment and that it is working. If the patient was referred to the practice, why not ask them who the referrer was and then not only have you got someone in common, but you can also send the referrer a thank you card or even a small gift. Marcos White, from Courtyard Dental Practice in Huddersfield, has an excellent reputation in his practice on the back of referrals and if he finds out who introduced his client, he will send a thank you card or maybe a plant or flowers.

If the patient says that they came to you via a website search, then another good question to ask is:

Mr Patient, do you mind me asking what was it about our website that caused you to contact us?

This is a great question because you can find out what is working on your website and what the patient likes. This again is useful information for the marketing of your practice.

So, at this stage we have established the patient's current situation and we have a platform to build on. The patient has informed us where they are now, what they are happy with and if there is anything they would like to change. Now, at this stage, most dentists start prescribing a solution and jump into providing a solution. If you do this then you could be making the cardinal sin of providing a solution to the patient without understanding what their wants and needs are. On my travels to dental practices, I often hear patients enquiring about teeth whitening and then I hear the dentist launch into the procedure. You can read more about this in the next chapter.

I once heard a statement that has lived with me for many years. It has kept me in good stead and I preach it to my clients regularly. "**Prescription before diagnosis is malpractice**". What I mean by this is that you offer a solution to your patient without first finding out what their wants and needs are. If you do this, it's malpractice, you risk offering the wrong solution, which, as I have already mentioned, is the biggest mistake dentists make on a daily basis.

So what we now need to do is move onto what we call **desired situation questions**. These tell us what the patient would ideally like to get out of their treatment. There are many advantages of asking these questions. The patient tells you what their ideal situation is, what their goals are and, as dentists, it will help you establish the patient's endgame. It makes it easier for us to prescribe the correct solution to the patient's issues.

Examples of these questions are

Mrs Patient, if you had a magic wand, what would you like your smile to look like at the end of treatment?

What would your ideal situation be?

Are you looking for a Hollywood smile, or somewhere in the middle?

Describe a perfect 10?

These are vital and important questions to ask as it stops us from making assumptions and we can prescribe the correct solutions to our patient's issues.

The third set of questions we ask are called **implication** questions and in short, these are questions where we get our patients to elaborate in more detail why they want the treatment. I often call these questions the "why now" questions. It helps us understand in a bit more detail why they are having the treatment, in other words the emotional reasons. I will go into more detail on the emotional reasons shortly.

Examples of these questions are:

Mr Patient, do you mind me asking what has caused your interest in having this treatment done now?

Why now?

Have you an event coming up where this new smile is important to you?

You said it is preventing you from smiling, do you mind sharing with me in what sort of situations you find this happening?

What impact is this having on your daily life?

These are important questions which clarify their issues and why they are not happy.

I find there are two motivators in life, towards motivation and away motivators. Let me give you an example.

I find people tend to take action more quickly when they are dissatisfied with their present situation. Let me give you an example and it is to do with gym membership. Please stick with me here as it has some relevance and makes a point.

Having belonged to a gym for many years, I find there are four major reasons why people tend to join a gym. These, in no particular order, include:

1. After Christmas/New Year's resolution - a lot of people join a gym after Christmas for the obvious reason that they have eaten and drunk too much and have put on weight, they join the gym to lose weight and feel good.

2. When booking a holiday - I find when people book a holiday, they might start visiting the gym because they are unhappy with their present situation and how they look, they want to get fit and lose weight so that they look good on the beach.

3. Getting divorced or splitting from a partner - someone joins a gym to create a new person, look good/feel good and even to meet new people. For ladies it is a safe environment to go on their own.

4. Health reasons - in other words the doctor has said that they must join a gym, because they have health problems.

In all these four circumstances the person is not happy with their present situation which makes them take action quickly and do something about it. I find that people tend to take action more quickly when they are not happy.

Implication questions are when you are asking more information about their current situation and the patient tells you in more detail why they are not happy. Let me share an example with you:

Neil Sampson, a dentist from Stafford, recalled a story. He was visited by an existing patient of many years and he asked her if there was anything that she was unhappy with or wanted changing. She answered she was not happy with the gap in her front teeth and also their colour. He went on to ask further questions and discovered that her daughter was getting married in six months' time. It was her only daughter and the reception was in a castle with over 250 guests coming from all over the world. She was worried about the photographs and also she was apprehensive about greeting the guests at the reception. This would not have been an issue six months earlier, but it was now and was becoming increasingly an issue as the big day got nearer and nearer. Neil found this out because he was genuinely interested and the patient volunteered this information. His questioning resulted in a £1,500 treatment plan as the patient also had her teeth whitened.

What is also interesting about this story is that it is important to keep asking your patients questions, as people's circumstances are changing all the time. My friend recently got divorced and found himself dating again. He decided that he would have his teeth straightened as he was unhappy with his crooked smile. This was not an issue, a few months earlier when he was married.

At this stage we have now asked current situation questions, desired situation questions and implication questions. The last set of questions we ask are the **what's-in-it-for-me** questions. These questions are exactly what it says on the tin. In other words, what are the advantages and benefits the patient will receive? The patients start to tell us their emotional reasons once they have achieved their goals.

Examples of these questions:

Mrs Patient, so if we were to straighten your teeth, what difference do you feel it will make for you?

What impact do you feel this will have once your teeth are a lot whiter?

What would it mean to you?

There are many advantages to asking these questions. These include:

1.  The patients start telling you the benefits of the treatment
2.  It becomes their idea, in which case they are more likely to buy and you will get fewer objections
3.  The patient is selling it to themselves
4.  They will share with you their emotional reasons for having the treatment.

Let's look at the emotional reasons in more detail.

A question I ask audiences all the time is this:

When people purchase products or services do they do it using logic or emotion?

The answer is both. There is always a logical reason to do something, but, on most occasions, there is an emotional reason as well. If, ladies, you don't believe me, go upstairs and count how many pair of shoes you have and label them if they were bought logically or emotionally.

Last year I changed my telephone from a basic Nokia telephone to a Blackberry, which had email. There were a few reasons why I changed. One of them was because my telephone was getting a little battered and worn. It was so old fashioned and outdated that my friends found it hilarious. However, there was a major reason why I needed to change my telephone and that was because I needed to get access to email instantly. I work away a lot and increasingly those nights away were getting longer, it is now not unusual for me to go away on a Sunday and not come home till Friday. So getting access to my email was important to my business and also for communicating with my clients. The other major advantage and the major reason why I changed the telephone was because when I was at home, I spent less time emailing and I had more time to spend with my family. When you are away so much, time with your family is paramount. The emotional reason why I changed my telephone was so that I could spend more time with my wife and children. That is very important to me.

If you ask these questions in order as I have recommended in this book, then you will be able to find out:

1. The major reason why someone is having treatment
2. The buying criteria which are essential for the products
3. The emotional reasons, which is always the why.

So let's go back to my telephone example.

The major reason why I wanted to change my telephone was to improve my communication with my clients. The telephone had to have email, look good and be easy to use. The emotional reasons why I wanted the telephone were because I wanted to spend more time with my family at home.

There are other emotional reasons why patients buy treatment and I will go through a few of these reasons with you. They include:

**Self Confidence**. If I have a nicer smile, then it will give me more self-confidence in social or work situations

**Keep up with the Jones's** Patients buy things because their peers have had something done and they want to keep up with them. It is the "in" thing.

**Survival** Let's say a patient has bleeding gums and it is causing their breath to smell then it might be affecting their performance at work, so it might be essential so that they keep their job.

The beauty of asking these questions is that you will ascertain all this information and it will help you later on when you are in the solution part of the process. In other words, you will be able to tailor your presentation to the patient's agenda without talking technical jargon, which has no relevance to what the patient is looking for. You will also be able to truly understand what your patient's wants and needs are and what is important to them in their solution. It will stop you from making assumptions and assuming what you think the patient wants.

Let's see things from the patient's point of view. They will be delighted that you took the trouble to build rapport and that you were genuinely interested in them as a person. Have you ever been shopping where the sales person took their time to truly understand your requirements and listen attentively and not try and sell you something? It very rarely happens. I often hear that patients shop around a lot nowadays. This was brought home when I heard this story from Chaw Su Kyi, an orthodontist in London.

Chaw Su Kyi is a client of mine and, after taking one of my courses, she related a story that had a great impact on me. Chaw was visited by a middle-aged patient who wanted orthodontic treatment. Chaw followed the above protocol to the letter. She spent time building rapport with the patient; she asked lots of open questions and listened attentively to the patient. At the end of the appointment the patient decided to undergo treatment with her. She then went on to tell Chaw that this was the third practice she had visited and the reason why she went ahead with her was because Chaw was the only orthodontist who spent time building rapport with her, got to know as a person and was genuinely interested in her wellbeing. In the other practices, she had felt like a number and not a person, and was rushed throughout the whole journey.

I often get asked by clients what they can do to stand out from the crowd. One way of standing out from the other dentists and orthodontists is to spend time building rapport, become genuinely interested in your client by asking lots of questions about their wants and needs. If you want patients to become genuinely interested in you, you must first become genuinely interested in them.

If you are going to be good at questioning, then listening to what your clients tell you is going to be absolutely paramount to the success of the consultation. I am going to spend several pages on listening skills, as I honestly believe it is the most important skill you can possess. If the consultation does not go well, it could be due to poor listening.

The name of the game here is deep listening. Deep listening is when we not only listen to the answers, but we are also listening to the client's feelings and their emotions. Listening to the words is important, but listening to the feelings is just as important, if not more important.

There are several types of listening and please read through the list and their explanations and see which one applies to you.

## Listen to Ignore

Listening to ignore is exactly what it says. You are listening but not taking anything in at all and not really interested in what the person is saying.

## Listening Selectively

Listening selectively is often known as 'man-type' listening, although many women say that there is not much difference between listening selectively and listening to ignore. Listening selectively is when you listen to what you want to hear and ignore the rest. I often use the example of when a man comes home from work and his partner tells him about their day, the price of food in the shops, or maybe a little tittle-tattle, stuff that is of real importance to the partner, but of little interest to the man who ends up saying things like: "Yes, dear", "Is that so, dear?". Then she says that she has booked a holiday and she needs a cheque for £5,000. All of sudden you become interested, because the price of the holiday is more than you expected.

## Listening like a Politician

Politicians often have to meet and greet hundreds of people, especially at election time. Listening like a politician is when you listen with a nice smile and grin. You might never meet the people you are listening to again, so you give them a grin and a smile. Politicians can be guilty of undertaking this type of listening as they can often be found to be nodding their head in agreement but the real question is are they truly listening?

## Listening Initially

Listening initially is when you start to listen to your patient and you are listening attentively at the start and then all of a sudden you drift and start thinking about something else and you totally lose track of what the patient, or colleague, has said. You then try and join back into the conversation, but realize that you have missed quite a bit and you find it hard to get back into the conversation.

## Listening to Respond

I am going to give this quite a bit of space because I feel it is an area that needs a lot of attention and I believe a lot of dentists listen like this.

Listening to respond is when you listen to the patient and then you start thinking what you are going to say and, when there is a space, or the other person has stopped speaking, you jump straight in with your answer. The problem with that type of listening is that:

1.   You don't really listen because you are already formulating an answer in your head. It is impossible to do both.
2.   You may offer the wrong solution to the patient's wants and needs
3.   The patient will feel that you have not listened and thus will feel cheated by your answers.

As I have already stated, not offering the solution to the patient's wants and needs is the biggest mistake sales people make.

## Listening Attentively

This type of listening is when we are solely focused on what the other person is telling us, we have no pre-conceived ideas and we are listening to the patient's emotions, as well as their words, we are genuinely interested and we go back with more questions such as:

Mrs Patient, tell me more.

Can you please tell me what you actually mean?

How often does that happen?

You are 100% focused on the patient's wants and needs and listening attentively, you are not thinking of any answers in your head.

This is the type of listening we need to aim for. This is the bull's eye and when we can listen at this level then it means that we can offer the correct solutions and also the patient feels that they have been heard and you will build strong relationships to move forward.

One way to listen attentively is to take notes, or even to get your nurse to take notes so that you do not miss anything in the consultation. This is also a great way of getting your nurse involved and enables them to be part of the process. They may hear something that you missed.

A person that is truly brilliant at listening is Michael Parkinson. Michael was the best interviewer in the UK for over 40 years, he interviewed thousands of stars from all over the world. He was a world class interviewer who always did his research and was an excellent listener.

More quick tips on your listening:

1.  Don't finish off your patient's sentences for them. If you ask a question, then listen carefully to the answer and do not put words in their mouths. Let the patient take ownership of the answer and not you.
2.  It is okay if there is a quiet part in the conversation. It basically means that the client is thinking, so please do not fill the space. Quiet times are okay.
3.  Summarize back to the patient when they have finished. This is one of the greatest tips I can share with you. If you have finished asking questions and you have all the information you need, then why not summarize back to the patient what they have told you. It goes something like this:

Mrs Patient, let me see if I have understood what you said.

Mr Patient, my understanding is that you want....

Then you relay back to the patient what they said using their own words. There are many advantages of using summaries. It will impress the client, because they feel that they have been understood, especially if you use their own words. The other thing it does is that if the patient at the end says yes, that's right, then it shows that the relationships between you and the patient is at a different level.

During this consultation, you should be listening for at least 80% of the time, the other 20% asking questions, or offering solutions, which I will cover in the next chapter. I once heard a great saying that the more you learn, the more you earn. In other words, the more information you can gather, the more you will earn. It used to be said that the best sales people are the ones with the gift of the gab. Although good, polished communication skills are vital, it is the people that can listen well who are the ones that will prosper the most. Stephen Covey in his excellent book "Seven Habits of Highly Effective People" states '**seek first to understand and then be understood.**' From the bible: "He who speaks without listening, that is their folly and shame" Proverbs18: 13 King Solomon.

The interesting thing is that people know when you are not really listening. I often would come home from work, shattered, and ask my kids about their day and, while they answered, watch the TV, especially if there was sport on. I would often get grief from them, and quite rightly so. If I spend the day with my kids, I often might not take my telephone with me, or if I do take it with me I will only answer it if it is a very important call. I do not make business calls when I am out with my family.

People often ask me to how you become a good listener. The only advice I can give you is to work at it. Make a note to become genuinely interested in people; if you want to become interesting, then you need to become interested. Patients do not care how much you know until you demonstrate how much you care and you can only do that by becoming genuinely interested. It is a skill that needs to be worked on and given constant attention. This is not an easy exercise to do, but why don't you ask your partner, or the person who is closest to you, what you are like as a listener and where you could improve? When they tell you, don't forget to listen, and do not interrupt.

Hopefully by now you have seen the major benefits of building rapport, asking questions and deep listening. There is one other major advantage and that is you won't make the other common mistake, you won't make assumptions.

Have you ever pre-judged a client by the way they look, are dressed or maybe by their post code? If you have, then please read on and I will share a few real life stories with you so that you will never make this mistake again.

Let me share a true story that happened only recently. I was booked by a client to deliver a two-day programme in London and I met the client the night before the programme for dinner. I asked my client what was the driving force behind wanting to take my course and why she wanted the whole team to take it. She went on to relate a story that blew me away.

She was visited by a regular patient who was 72 years of age and had recently been widowed. The patient was not happy with her dentures and wanted them replacing. They were loose and she could not chew her food properly and didn't like the look of them. The dentist prescribed eight more dentures and the patient said that she would think about it and come back to her. The dentist did not hear anything for a few months until her next appointment when, to the dentist's horror, she discovered that the patient had eight implants fitted at another practice. When the dentist found out why she went elsewhere to get the treatment done, it was because the patient did not think that the dentist could do the procedure. She had seen an advert in a magazine and went to Harley Street to have the treatment. The dentist had trained for many years to fit implants and, because of the patient's age, had presumed that she would not want implants, and also that she could not afford them. The dentist lost an opportunity to fit eight implants and an income of around £15,000. How many practices can afford to lose this sort of case?

Only recently a dentist in Ireland had a visit from a new client who came into the surgery with four young children. He noticed that she was dressed quite scruffily and labelled her a single mum on benefits. The woman started talking about some expensive treatment she wanted to have done, and the dentist got a shock when he discovered she was a surgeon in the local hospital.

Ashish Parmar told me once about a patient who was a window cleaner who was getting married in a few months' time and how he hated his smile. He went on to say how much he hated his dentures and that he was dreading his wedding photographs. Ashish presented him with a treatment plan totalling £16,000, the client came back a few hours later and paid a deposit in cash.

One of my favourite stories was from Neil Sampson. On a very wet November evening he was visited by a traveller, who walked into his practice with two black eyes, a broken nose and two missing teeth. He had been involved in a fight, the wrong place at the wrong time, and as a result had lost two front teeth. Neil put into practice everything he had learned from my course. He found out, from building rapport and deep questioning, that the guy wanted his original teeth back and wanted implants to replace his missing teeth. Neil quoted a price of over £4,000 and got a shock when the patient paid for the treatment in cash. Neil honestly did not think he had ten pence to his name.

So, if you spend time building rapport with your patients, and ask them lots of questions, the major benefit is that it will stop you from making assumptions.

The other advantages are that you will take your relationship to another level; you will probably create more opportunities as your patients will tell you what they would like to have done, and you should get less price resistance and fewer objections.

## Things to do
1. Take time to build rapport with your patient. Have a chat with your patient before you put them in the dental chair.
2. Ask your patients questions about their health and appearance. There are literally thousands of pounds worth of treatment plans sitting in your patients' heads, you just need to ask them questions.
3. Practice becoming a great listener. Ask your colleagues where you can improve as a listener. Make sure you listen carefully to the answers.
4. Remember if you want to become interesting, then you need to become interested.

In the next chapter, I am going to share with you some common mistakes dentists make when presenting treatment and by changing your language how you can help more of your patients to say yes more often.

Chapter Four:

# Providing a Unique Solution

So far in the sales process, we have built rapport, asked questions, listened attentively to the client and summarized back to them what their issues are. The next step in the process is to provide a solution.

If you are a dentist or an orthodontist and you are reading this, I have some news that might upset you. In fact, life will never be the same again after this chapter.

If you are an orthodontist, I am not sure your patients are interested in the fact that the treatment you are suggesting is made up of *"passive self-ligating brackets which have low frictional forces using heat activated niti wires containing 6% copper"*.

Or, if you are a dentist speaking to your patients and you tell them that: *"an implant is a titanium screw is surgically screwed into your jawbone under anaesthetic"*.

I am certain that when you talk too technical, then it can confuse the patient and probably put them off having treatment. Only the other week, one of my friends suggested that I buy a certain camera, with an inbuilt video, which would be good to use on my programmes. I went to a camera shop in Manchester to enquire about it. The sales person brought the camera out and then proceeded to give me a five-minute technical spiel using jargon that put me off. To be honest, I felt stupid, as I did not know or understand the words that he was using. At the end when he asked me if I had any questions, I said I did not and left the shop highly confused, without making a purchase.

I see this all the time in practices, when a patient enquires about tooth whitening and then the receptionist, or the dentist replies:

"Well, we have two ways of delivering the treatment.

We will alginate impressions to make study models on which we construct custom-made bleaching trays made from vacuum-formed polyurethane trays. You will place 15% car amide peroxide which is a bleaching gel into the trays which you wear every night for a month.

The other way is that you can sit in the chair for two hours, wear protective spectacles, gum round your gums, so that you don't get black laser light, and we'll apply three lots of bleach to your teeth at 15-minute intervals. If you feel your gums are burning, we will apply vitamin E lotion to stop the burning."

Maybe I am going over the top here, but I often hear something similar, full of jargon. I have devoted several pages to this topic later in the book.

Imagine that you have broken down on the motorway. It is a Friday night, it is raining, cold and you are still a hundred miles away from home. Imagine the engineer appears and looks at your problem and, before he starts, he asks you to come into the back of his van whilst he gives you a 45-minute presentation on his tools and how they all work. Alternatively, you are in a restaurant and you order a steak, and the chef comes to your table and gives you an explanation on how old the cow was, how it was killed and what they did to get onto your plate. Would you be interested?

I can understand why dentists sometimes talk too technical, after all you are a technical profession and this is what you were taught. I am often told that there is very little training or coaching on communication skills at dental school. Only last year, a dentist openly admitted that he had put off taking my programme for 3 years, whilst he went on lots of technical courses. He also admitted that he believed that the more technical he talked to the patients, the more they would believe him, and the more they would go ahead with the treatment he offered. He quickly discovered after taking my two-day programme that he had in fact spent three years confusing his patients and he could see why patients were not taking up his treatment plans.

In this chapter, I will give you an insight into the type of language you can use to excite the patient about what you offer, the importance of evidence.

I have found that people don't often buy the features of a product or service, they buy what the product or service will do for them. In other words, the benefits. You see on the whole people are only interested in what's in it for them. Have a review of the products and services that you have recently purchased and see why you bought them and you will probably note that you purchased the benefits.

I am about to buy an iPad for the simple reason that I spend so much time on the road, I want to improve my communication with my clients. In fact this is essential to the success of my business.

I would urge you when you are communicating to see things from the other person's point of view, wear their shoes and not yours. I once heard a great expression, which was K.I.S.S. - keep it simple stupid.

Let's get into the structure of your patient presentation.

## Features

Everyone knows what features are. They are facts, data or information about the product or service. Examples of features are:

We are open Saturday morning 8.30am till 12.30pm every week.

We have a 0% finance package and you can spread the payments interest free over 6 months.

All these are features or facts. Features on their own are unpersuasive. As I said before: patients are interested in buying benefits.

## Benefits

There can be several definitions of a benefit, but my definition is: how a feature can help a patient. It is what they will gain by using your feature. For example, let's link some benefits to the above features.

Feature: We are open every Saturday morning 8.30am till 12.30pm.

Benefit: You don't need to take any time off work.

Feature: We have a 0% finance package and you can spread the payments over 6 months interest free.

Benefit: You can start the treatment today.

One of the recurring problems my dental clients tell me they have is that they sometimes have an issue with people cancelling their appointments with the hygienist.

If you tell your patients that they need to visit the hygienist because they will give you a scale and polish, or they will clean your teeth for you, don't be too surprised if patients don't turn up for their appointments. It is not a major benefit.

However, if you say something like: Our hygienist will educate and treat your gums, the benefit is that you are likely to keep your teeth a lot longer and it will reduce the chances of you getting gum disease.

I am not saying that this statement will totally eliminate all your cancellations, but I am certain it will reduce the number, your patients will see a clear benefit and the importance of visiting the hygienist.

So far we have used the language of features and benefits. Another piece of communication we can tag onto a benefit is often known as an advantage or, a definition that works well for me, a **what's-in-it-for-me statement**. This, in short, is when you tell the patient what the benefit of the benefit is, in others words what it will allow them to do.

This is not an easy concept to get across and the best way to explain this is to continue with the illustration above.

For the purpose of this example, imagine you have a client who is interested in having a course of treatment done, but is finding it challenging to get into the practice because of work commitments. Here is how you can present your case to the patient:

## Feature
We are open every Saturday 8.30am till 12.30pm.

## Benefit
Is that you will not miss any work

**Which means** because you are not missing any work, you can concentrate on the project you were telling me about and have that lovely smile for the presentation that you are doing in three weeks time.

Here is the other example:

Let's imagine the patient wants to proceed with a course of treatment with you, but they cannot afford to pay the bill all at once and they have a wedding to go to in a few weeks' time. The patient is worried about smiling in photographs.

**Feature:** we have a 0% finance scheme in place at the practice.

**Benefit** is that you can start the treatment today

**Which means** that you will be able to smile in the photographs at your daughter's wedding in a few weeks time.

The final statement, which I have titled the 'which means', normally addresses the emotional reasons why the patients buy and that is why I consider them to be very powerful and persuasive statements.

Can you see the difference and the impact it can have?

Hopefully now our patient is excited about taking up our proposal, and to check that we are on the right track, we can use a statement which we call the 'test close'. A test close is a non-threatening question, where we are gauging the patient's reaction to what we have discussed with them. It is normally a question that goes like:

Mrs Patient, how does this sound?

Is that what you are looking for?

I find a lot of dentists find it difficult to close the treatment plan. By using this statement, you can see if you are on the right track and whether the patient is happy with what you have discussed with them. Please do not confuse this question with a close, it is a test close. I will cover closing in more detail in a later chapter.

My clients tell me that test closes really work, because they are like little stepping stones to the acceptance of the plan and it makes it easier to get to the commitment stage.

There are many advantages of following this structure. These include:

1. It stops the waffle
2. The language is the patient's and not your own
3. It is persuasive
4. It stops you talking too technical
5. Hopefully it will reduce the number of objections you get from your patients
6. It motivates the patient to move forward

Now that we have used the language of features and benefits, this leads to another very powerful strategy we can use – evidence. Before I share with you my thoughts on the different types of evidence that you can use, let me share a personal story with you.

A few weeks ago I decided to go for a run. I had the evening planned, I was going to come back to a hot bath and then settle down to watch some TV. As I left the house, my wife Graziella was on the computer reading customer feedback on a couple of vacuum cleaners that she was interested in buying. When I came back about an hour later, guess what, she was still on the computer reading these reviews and she stayed on for a further 20 minutes. Three things really hit home to me. These were:

1. People read customer feedback before making a decision on purchasing something

2.   The power of evidence and the importance of having good feedback from your clients
3.   People will spend a long time reading up before making a decision to buy something. My wife spent the best part of two hours researching to make a £250 purchase.

So, if people are influenced by reviews and testimonials, how can we take this concept and apply it to dentistry?

Let's look at evidence and some examples of what we can use.

## Testimonial Letters

On my courses, one of the things I encourage dentists and their staff to do is to collect testimonial letters from happy and delighted patients. Often at the start of the conversation it gets the thumbs down until we explore the concept in more detail. A testimonial letter is a letter from a patient who has taken the trouble to write to you to say how happy they have been with the treatment and the service they have received and also the benefits they have now gained.

The best way of collecting your testimonial letters is to ask your patients. At first there can be some reluctance from the practice team and this could be because:

1.   They lack the self-confidence to ask
2.   It's new and people are sometimes sceptical about doing something new
3.   They feel that the patient will say no
4.   They are worried about patient confidentiality.

All these reasons are all pretty valid, however, let's look at the advantages, and there are many. They include:

1.  It gives patients confidence in your work
2.  It will reduce the objections that you receive
3.  If you leave the testimonials in the reception area, they let patients know what you do and might promote some of your services
4.  It just might encourage the patient to enquire about your services when they come into the surgery.

It has to be better than the patients reading the paper or magazines, which may contain competition to the services you provide. By the way, I am not saying that you should completely move all your magazines and newspapers, but please make sure that you have some of your own stuff out there so people can read about what you do.

You just need to feel comfortable in asking so that you can obtain a book of these letters. Here is an example of how to ask:

Mrs Jones, I wonder if I could ask you a small favour please?

I wonder if you could help us to help other patients. Often we get asked for a reference for patients who are unsure about going ahead with treatment, usually because they are nervous. I wondered if you could please write a short testimonial letter for us, stating the benefits you have gained from the treatment, so that we could show this to these nervous patients?

Now you can ask the patient to write it there and then at the desk, or give them a pre-paid envelope to take home with them to post back to you.

I also suggest that you place these on your website and ensure they are visible on your front page. Better still, video your clients and get some verbal testimonials and again place them on the front page of your website. As a side issue, Google likes video on your website and it will help you if you are doing search engine optimization.

The other thing a book of testimonial letters can do for you is give you a little gee up when you feel a little down. A quick read of the letters from your happy clients can give you a quick boost and put you back in the right frame of mind for your day.

Here is an example of a letter you could ask your patient to fill in with a view to using their testimonial in your practice, on your website and social media

### +++++ put your logo/letterhead here++++

### Permission Letter for Publishing Video Testimonials or Photographs on the website or on Social Media

Dear

I would like to request your permission for either a video testimonial or your photographs to be used on our website and marketing. This means third parties would be able to view the photographs and your quotes.

If you sign the attached form it means that you agree to the following:

1. _____ are able to publish your testimonial and/or your photograph as many times as it requires in the ways mentioned above.

2. The clinic will not use your testimonial or photograph for any purpose other than for the website or for the general promotion.

3. _____ will not resell the material to any third parties without your consent.

If you agree to permit the clinic to produce a video testimonial and photographs to be published please complete this consent form.

## Consent

I agree to the shooting of a video testimonial and the taking of photographs for the use by _____ to promote the clinic.

I will notify the clinic if I decide to withdraw this consent.

**Name of client:**

**Signature of client:**

**Date:**

## Before and After Pictures

This is so simple to do. Buy a good digital camera and start taking some before and after pictures of your patients' teeth before zthey had treatment and after. Put the pictures in a nice album strategically placed in the reception area. It might also be beneficial to have copies in the surgery and/ or consultation room. If you have them in the reception area your patients will review the pictures and it might encourage them to ask questions about what is possible for them. It also gives them confidence in your work. I know a couple of practices I have visited which have a few pictures of their clients in nice picture frames on the walls around the practice. Again this gives your patients confidence. You obviously must ask for permission from your patients.

As a side issue, these photographs could be given to your clients at the end of treatment so they can see the difference you have made. I know some dentists who place these in nice folders with their logo on, it makes a nice gift for the patient. They will hopefully show this to their friends and relatives and it might bring new patients to your door.

## Success Stories

Sharing success stories with your patients is another way of boosting your credibility. This is when you give an example of another patient who went ahead with your treatment and you share with the patient the major benefits they have gained since having the treatment done by you. Please ensure that you do not mention names, unless you have permission, and that the story that you are sharing is relevant to the person you are speaking to.

## Demonstration

Sometimes it is necessary to demonstrate the product or service that you are going to provide. For example, if you are an orthodontist it might be a good idea to show examples of the braces that you are going to use. People like to feel, touch and see what it is they are buying and demonstrations work a treat.

## Facts and Figures

Sometime you might need to build credibility. You can inform the patients of your track record by perhaps quoting figures on how many procedures you have delivered to back up your verbal presentation. This gives your patients re-assurance. For example, the fact that I have now delivered my two-day Ethical Sales & Communication Programme to well over 8,000 delegates in the last 18 years gives my clients' confidence in what I do.

## Computer Imaging

This form of evidence is very popular. Here digital photographs are modified to show the various possibilities of different aesthetic approaches to create a new smile. The main advantage is that the patient can have an idea of what the end result is likely to be, and in some cases, have a say. As the client can see the potential end result, this can be a very powerful form of evidence.

I strongly suggest that you get your team on board and work together putting evidence in to place within your practice. They will help co-ordinate all this and probably come up with more ideas than are mentioned in this book.

## Things to do

1. If you are a dentist or an orthodontist, ask your team members if you talk using too much technical information. Ask them to be honest with you and to share examples of what you say or do.

2. At the same time ask them if you waffle. If so, again ask them to give you examples and discuss ways in which you can improve.

3. Get into the habit of talking benefits and the language that your patient understands.

4. Make sure that the whole practice talks the same language and is singing off the same hymn sheet.

5. Collect your evidence and create folders. Ask your patients for testimonial letters and create a file of before and after pictures.

6. Strategically place some after pictures in the surgery in nice picture frames. It looks attractive and you might just create more opportunities for the practice. For example, if you are in an orthodontic practice and deliver lots of treatment to children, ensure that you have pictures of adults in the practice, as you will create adult opportunities.

Chapter Five:
# Overcoming Objections & Reducing Doubt

So far you have built strong rapport, asked good questions, provided a solution in tune with the patient's agenda and, of course, you have shown them some evidence. You believe the patient is excited and is ready to buy and, all of a sudden, they throw an objection at you and you start to crumble. It could be about price, time or even your opening hours and you become tongue-tied and unsure what to do next. This chapter will look at the big mistakes dentists and orthodontists make when they meet objections. You will learn what to say and, just as important, what not to say, and also how to successfully overcome your patients' objections to create a win-win.

When I deliver my two-day programme, many delegates tell me that the material I am about to share with you is life-changing and that they benefit significantly from this material. In my opinion, successfully overcoming objections is not easy and can be a challenging part of the sales process. So, before we look at overcoming objections, let's define what an objection is and why we get them.

An objection is a barrier to the sale and, if you don't acknowledge them and overcome your patients' concerns, then the sale cannot proceed. If we put a positive slant on it, an objection can also be a request for more information and a sign that the patient is still keen to proceed, but they have a concern that needs addressing.

There can be several reasons why you might get an objection from your clients. It may be they have pre-conceived ideas, or they have heard something negative from a friend. However, the most likely reason is because of something that you have done in the previous part of the sales process. For example, it may be because you did not ask enough questions, or did not explain the treatment options well and the patient is unsure. Many clients who have taken my two-day course tell me that once they become an expert at building rapport, asking questions and providing solutions, they tend to get fewer objections and in some cases they don't get any at all.

One of the biggest mistakes I find dentists, or in fact the thousands of sales people I have trained during my career make when they get an objection is that they get defensive. When they receive an objection, they take it personally. This is a big no-no. If you get defensive, not only will you end up saying the wrong thing, but it can also have an impact on the relationship with your client. Let's look at the common defensive statements people say, for example:

"That seems a high price", or "that's expensive".

To which I often hear the response: "No, it isn't", "It's a good investment," "It will last a long time".

There are more.

Please let me share with you an analogy on what happens when you get defensive and you start taking objections personally. Have you ever had situation at home where your partner gives you a ticking off for something that you have done? On hearing them shout at you, you start to get defensive about your situation. Before you know it, the argument gets more intense; she gets her gun out, you get your machine gun, she throws a bomb and you get into your tank. Before you know it, one hell of a mighty row is in place, which leads to you both not speaking for two days. Now I'm sure that this has not happened to you. This is what can happen if you get defensive about your own situation. If you do this at work then you might get your patient's back up and it will impact on the relationship.

So, if you get an objection the first thing you need to do is to put yourself in your patient's shoes. See things from their point of view and see why they have a concern. In other words, you need to take your shoes off and put their shoes on. If you do then you will be able to deal with the objection better.

The other mistakes I often hear people make is as they listen to the objection from the patient but will butt in and try to answer the patients' concerns before the patient has even finished. This can happen if the dentist has heard the objection many times, so they make assumptions about the objection, another mistake. The patient feels that you haven't listened to their concerns and feels cheated. Even if you are dealing with an objection that you have heard before, please ensure that you deal with it as it were the first time you'd heard it.

Being an outstanding listener is absolutely paramount here and you must ensure that you listen attentively to what the patient is saying, not just listening to their words, but also to the feelings behind their words, and ensure that you let the patient finish everything that they have to say. In previous chapters, I stated that giving the patients a prescription before the diagnosis is malpractice, and this is more important now in dealing with the patients' objections.

Before I go through the five steps approach that will help you overcome objections, one thing that you need to understand is that it is impossible to overcome every objection. This is my disclaimer and let me tell you why. Let's say a patient wants orthodontic treatment and their teeth straightened in three months and you know for a fact that it will take 12 months. If the patient is adamant, then there is not a lot you can do. If a patient wants teeth whitening and your treatment costs £475 and they only want to pay half that amount, then it is going to be impossible to make the sale. However, if you follow the steps I am going to share with you, then you should increase the chance of overcoming objections.

So, once we have listened attentively and the patient has finished then you go to step one:

## Step One: Build empathy
Let's say a patient has given you a price objection, you build empathy by using the following statement:

Mr Patient, I understand that you have a concern with the price of the treatment.

Mrs Patient, I understand that you may have a concern over the level of investment.

Mr Patient, it is perfectly normal to have that concern, after all it is the first time you have had this level of treatment for many years.

When you use this type of statement you are demonstrating to your patient that you fully understand their concerns. At this stage we are not answering the objection, we are not agreeing with the patient nor are we disagreeing with them, just acknowledging their concerns. There are many advantages to building empathy. The patient feels that they have been listened to and that you are taking what they say seriously. This is important to the relationship and the patient will most likely take on board your ideas when you answer the objection. It also gives us time to think what we are going to say back to the patient. One final tip here, try and avoid saying things like:

You are not the first person to say that the treatment is expensive, or, I agree with you, it is expensive.

What you are doing here is agreeing with the patient and it might make it difficult to win them round.

So once we have built empathy, let's move on to step two:

**Step Two: Asking the patient for more information**
In this part of the process you are now asking your patient for more information about their objection so that you fully understand what their concerns are. This is vital to the process. Sometimes what people say, how we interpret it,

what they really mean, can often be completely different things. For example, let's take price again to make the point here. The patient gives you a price objection and says something like: 'That is expensive'.

The price objection can be many things. It maybe

1.  They cannot afford to have the treatment
2.  It might be that they want to know why it costs that much, in other words, they need more information
3.  They may have seen the treatment cheaper at another practice
4.  It may be cash flow and they might not have the money to pay for it all at once.

At this stage we might not be a 100% sure certain what the patient's objection is so by asking the question you can fully understand what the patient's concern is. Do not assume what it is, because you might end up addressing the wrong objection.

An example of the question you can ask is:

Mrs Patient, do you mind if I ask you a question? When you said that the treatment was expensive what is it you actually mean?

Or:

Mrs Patient, please give me a little more information about your concern with my price?

You then listen to the answer attentively and then clarify it back to the patient. Once you do this and you fully understand the objection, then you can move on to step three.

## Step Three: Ask if there is anything else?

This is when you ask the patient if they have any other concerns with the treatment? In other words, we are asking the patient if they have any other objections. This might seem a strange thing to do, because we are inviting more objections. It is hard enough dealing with the first one and here we are asking for more! The following story will help you understand why step three is vital to overcoming objections.

A few years ago I was introduced to a dentist who referred me to the managing director of the IT company who supported his practice. For the life of me I cannot remember his name, buts let's say it's John. John was superb at his job and the dentist was delighted with the support that he gave his practice and they had become good friends. However, John was not a good salesperson and he admitted that this was a weak link in his business. He openly admitted that he was a lousy negotiator, could not close deals and new appointments would often stress him out. I knew my course would not only help John, but it would also be a life changing experience for him. If this was not enough, he would also get the opportunity to network with at least 20 dentists on my course. With this in mind, John signed up to the programme.

A few days before the programme, we had not received John's paperwork or his cheque for the programme, so I duly rang him up. He told me that he could not afford to do the programme as he had just moved house and the costs were a lot more than he had budgeted for. I was stunned when I heard this as I knew he would get a significant return on his investment and that the programme would pay for itself several times over. So I asked him if he had any other concerns. He then went on to inform me that he did not want to do my programme, because he did not like role play and the thought of even standing up to say his name was making him feel nervous. As a side issue, that was the major reason why John needed to do my programme. On reflection of this conversation, his concern was not about the money, but the fact that my programme was interactive and that he would have to take part; this was his true concern. He did not tell me this at the start, as he was embarrassed and he used money as a smokescreen. That is why you need step three, to see if the client has any other concerns. If there are any other objections, then it could be that the second objection is the main one and that the first one, although important, is not as big as issue as the second one. So step three we ask the client if they have any other concerns. We now have all the objection(s) on the table and we are now ready to move to step four which is to answer the objection.

## Step Four: Provide information to overcome the objection

There are many ways to answer objections and I will give an explanation of each one.

1. Evidence

One of the best ways to overcome objections is to use evidence. These include all the evidence techniques that we covered in Chapter Four and can include:

Success stories
Testimonial letters
Facts and figures
Before and after photographs
Analogies

2. Explain and educate

Let's say that a patient has a concern that the treatment might hurt, or why it takes so long, in the example of orthodontic treatment, then you need to explain and educate your patient what happens and why it takes so long. Please ensure that when you explain here, you are doing this in layman terms.

3. Feel, felt, found

Feel, felt, found is an excellent way of overcoming patient's objections. In short, when you receive an objection from a patient, you state that you understand how they feel; many other patients felt the same way, however, they went ahead and this is what they found. The 'found' is the success story. This is a good technique to use, if the patient is say apprehensive or scared about having the treatment done.

4. Overcoming price objections

There can be many different versions of price objections and it is important that you use the questioning in step two to find out exactly what is their price concern. I will go through some of them and show you some suggested answers.

Cash Flow

If the patient hasn't the funds to pay for the treatment all at once, then you can offer a monthly payment plan. I suggest that you work out the monthly payments for them. It becomes even more attractive, if the payment plan is interest free

Why does it cost that much?

With this objection you need to explain and educate the patient why it costs so much and what is involved. When you do, please ensure that you are speaking in layman's terms. Let's say a patient is quibbling over the cost of a crown. They might think that you are literally opening a drawer and taking a crown out and fitting it into the mouth of the patient. Here you need to give a simple explanation that could be something like: we will make a temporary crown, and send the new crown to be designed and manufactured by a skilled technician, who will then send it back when we will check it and then fit the crown for you. This price covers the technician's costs and includes a 12-month guarantee. All of a sudden you have created value and you have educated your patient.

Cheaper elsewhere

This is an interesting objection and is becoming more frequent as people have started to shop around for their dental needs. The best way to overcome this objection is to find out more information on what they have been quoted and see if it is like for like. Once you have done that you then explain to the patient about your unique process and what you offer, or do that is different. Patients don't necessarily mind paying more, they just want to know what the difference is. A quick rule of thumb here is not to knock the competition, in my opinion it is very unprofessional. Focus on explaining the benefits that you provide.

## Step Five: The Test Close

Once you have overcome the patients' objections then you can swiftly move on to step five which is a test close. You ask the patient if they are happy with your answer and therefore comfortable with moving ahead. A test close is not a close, it is just a non-threatening question to check that the patient is happy with your answer. Examples of this are:

Have I answered your concern?

Do you feel happier now?

How does that sound?

If you get a positive answer then you can move on to the gaining commitment stage of the sales process, often known as closing, which I will explore in much detail in the next chapter.

If you follow these five steps, it should improve your skills and of course your chances of overcoming your patient's objections.

Again I want to repeat myself, it is not possible to overcome every single objection. I often have conversations with clients who inform me that they are now a lot more skilled than they were, but have still encountered stubborn patients where these communication skills did not work. It is impossible to overcome all objections. If it was, I would be a very rich man by now.

## Things to do

1. Review with your team some of the common objections that you receive in the Practice
2. Develop some scripts and practice with your whole team what to say when you get them from your patients
3. Have on-going conversations in your team meetings so that you can practice any new objections that you might get.
4. Anticipate what they might be and ensure that you have good evidence to back up what you communicate

Chapter Six:

# Talking Money with Confidence

On my courses, one of the biggest challenges my clients tell me that they want some help with is money. As well as overcoming money objections, they want help with all aspects of money, such as talking money and especially being confident in charging the prices their services deserve. I often hear stories of dentists who think of one price in their head and by the time it comes out of their mouth, the figure is less. Here are some thoughts, observations and tips that hopefully should make you feel more comfortable talking money with confidence.

1.  Is price an issue, or <u>the</u> issue?

Here is a simple exercise to do. Please write down three purchases that you recently made. It can be anything, a pair of shoes, trousers, dress, suit, camera, you have got the picture. Please ask yourself this question. When you purchased the item, was price the issue, or an issue? In other words, if price was the single major factor when you purchased the item, then please put a tick next to the item. I find when I do this exercise, that although price is important, it is very rarely the single major issue and there are other factors more important, such as brand, quality, service etc.

The single major lesson I would like you to take away is that price is very rarely the major factor when people buy things. Although you do get the odd person shopping around, I feel that patients tend not to shop around for dentistry, other factors than price are more important.

This is also a great exercise to do with the rest of your team. At a staff meeting do the same exercise and ask your team to write down three things that they recently purchased. Discuss between you if price was the single major factor when the purchase was made. You will probably find that only a few purchases were price driven.

2. Forget the 'screamers'

Have you ever had a situation when you have quoted a price to a patient and they came back with a response such as 'I suppose I'm paying for your car or holiday, am I?', and of course they are bellowing this out in a loud, cynical voice! It can often make you feel uncomfortable. I find that dentists tend to think that when they quote a price to a patient that all the patient is thinking is that they are being ripped off. The point I would like to emphasize is that you might only get a few of these 'screamers' a year, and that half of them are saying it in jest. My only advice is that you need to stop thinking about these patients and move on. If they take up room in your head, they win and I am certain it will influence the way you communicate to your next patient.

Only last year I had a situation where I was challenged very loudly, and in my view, rudely by a dentist during a presentation I was giving. The room was packed and this gentleman on two occasions stated that I was talking rubbish and he didn't agree with me. I have to say in 24 years of speaking all over the world, this was the first time this had ever happened, and it made me feel very uncomfortable. After my presentation I was physically sick as my stomach was knotted. I had this gentleman's face in my head for a week and it affected everything that I did, my self-confidence was at an all time low. After a week and a hard conversation with myself, I decided to move on and get over it. After all this was the first time this had ever happened and I had a proven track record with over 8,000 dental professionals taking my courses and literally hundreds of testimonial letters from clients telling me that I changed their lives and made a difference to their practices. So why was I letting one man ruin my life? I can safely say the following week; I was back to my normal self. Forget the screamers, if you don't they win.

3.   Communicate value

When quoting a price to the patient, instead of just saying the price, why don't you let the patient know what they get for their investment? For example, which statement seems convincing?

The price of your crown is £495.

Or

The price of your crown is £495 which includes your temporary crown and then we send it off to be made by a skilled laboratory technician who will design and then handcraft your crown to your requirements. When it comes back we will check it and then fit it for you and of course this includes a 12 month guarantee.

Do you see the difference between the two statements? I believe the second statement creates real value for money. Sometimes patients don't know what is involved in the procedure, maybe they think that a crown is just taken out of a drawer and popped into the patient's mouth. So by educating your patient on what is involved, you should eliminate objections from your patients.

4.  Are you Harrods, John Lewis or a car boot salesman?

For the purpose of this exercise, imagine I am in front of you holding a lacquered tea tray with an idyllic Lake District design on it. Imagine the tray is for sale in John Lewis or equivalent. How much would you expect to pay for the tray?

Now imagine you are walking around a car boot sale on a Sunday morning in your local town, how much is the tea tray now?

And finally Harrods in London, how much do you believe it is on sale for now?

When I do this exercise with my clients we get prices from anything from £3 for the car boot sale up to £550 for Harrods. The reason is pretty obvious. In Harrods you pay for the brand, customer service, the surroundings and experience.

What is the purpose of this exercise? Well, everything counts in your practice. If you want to charge higher prices for your services, then make sure that your customer service is world class, the patient journey is extraordinary and that the practice looks like a modern 21st century practice. Have you ever been to a restaurant where the food and service is good, but you visit the bathroom and it is a disaster zone? All of a sudden you start having nightmares thinking that if the bathroom is in this state, what is the kitchen like?

Let me share with you a true story that backs this up. A few years ago I ran one of my Two Day Ethical Sales & Communication Programmes in Manchester in a three star hotel in the centre of the town. The hotel has an excellent gym, which I've been a member of for over 15 years, and I decided to use the hotel's conference facilities to hold one of my courses. The programme went well and the feedback sheets were very positive, except one of the sheets which gave me poor feedback. The feedback was completely different to the other sheets; it was as if this person had taken part in another programme. I had a terrible night's sleep that night and I could not wait till the next morning to speak to the client to see why he was not happy.

I rang the client at 8.30am the next day. After a detailed discussion, the client confirmed that he was delighted with the course, loved the programme and the materials, but was disappointed with the hotel, food and the accommodation. He said something that has lived with me forever. He said: "Ashley, your course is brilliant, you are brilliant, but ensure you have a hotel that fits the brilliance of your programme." What a lesson and I never made the mistake again. That was the last time I used this particular hotel. It wasn't the course that he was upset about, but the hotel and the peripheries and that is what I believe your patients make judgments on. They cannot always judge the quality of your work, but they can judge the experience and the patient journey.

5.   The invisible product

Contrary to what you think, I honestly believe patients do not shop around for dentistry, I know a few do, but not everyone. Dentistry is an invisible purchase. In other words, if patients are buying cosmetic dentistry they are purchasing an end result and not something that is tangible. If, for example, you want to buy a certain camera or iPod, then you can go on line and compare the prices from different shops or stores. With dentistry, although you can get prices of a crown, it is the relationship and all the other things that are taken into consideration.

6.   You are worth it

Do you ever find when you are quoting a price that you start off with a price and by the time it comes out of your mouth, it is less than the price in your head? Why do dentists do this?

Dentists and orthodontists spend years at university/dental school so that you can become a doctor. You continue going on training programmes to update your knowledge, I know a lot of dentists do a lot more continued professional development than they need to. When I worked with the Dale Carnegie Training Organization, I spent many years being coached to be a trainer. Just to qualify to become a Dale Carnegie Trainer I had to go through over 500 hours of unpaid training. The training was tough, it was often said that it was like going through a SAS course. Then I had to go through the whole experience again to become an International Master Trainer. In addition, I have spent hundreds of thousands of pounds going on courses, reading books, listening to CD's to update my knowledge and skills. You do the same. As I am writing this section, I am reminded of the story of Pablo Picasso. He was having dinner in a restaurant in New York, when a lady came up to see him and commented that she was a big fan of his work. She asked if it was possible that he could draw her something there and then. He took a napkin and started to draw the waiters who were serving at the table. When he finished he handed the napkin to her and requested ten thousand dollars. On hearing this the lady was shocked and said "That it only took you 5 minutes" to which Picasso replied "No madam it took me a lifetime". As the L'Oreal advert says, you are worth it. Be proud of your prices and speak what is in your head.

7.   Quote investment not cost

Instead of saying the cost of the treatment, why not quote investment instead? With an investment you, hopefully, get something back in return, where a cost is something that costs you and you don't get anything back in return.

As I am writing this book I had a coaching conversation with a client who informed me that, because the dentist up the road had put his prices down on certain treatments, such as teeth whitening, she was doing the same. After a deep routed conversation, it soon became clear that she was making virtually no profit every time she delivered this procedure.

She even openly admitted that, having reduced her prices, there had been no increase in sales of teeth whitening. She asked me for my advice. I told her to double the price that she was charging and be more expensive than the person down the road, otherwise, if she carried on like this, she would go out of business. It brought home to me that price is very rarely the issue when people are buying services or products, and if something is too cheap, then people might not think it is any good.

## Things to do

1. Have a meeting with your team and ask them the three things they recently purchased and ask them if price was an issue when they bought them. Discuss your findings in more detail.
2. Remember price is only one issue, not the single major factor when patients buy things.
3. On the whole, patients do not shop around for dentistry.

In the next chapter, I am going to share with you the second biggest mistake dentists make. For a great percentage of my clients who take my programme; this is life-changing material.

Chapter Seven:

# Gaining Commitment

In the previous chapter I talked about the biggest mistake in sales: assuming what the patient required. In other words, offering a solution to the patient without first finding out what the patient required. After delivering sales and business training for over 24 years, I honestly believe that the second biggest mistake dentists make is not gaining commitment to the treatment plan, in other words, not closing. I also believe that this mistake is common in all industry sales.

Before I move on with this topic, I want to inform you that I am not into hard sales closing techniques and forcing treatment and products onto clients and patients. I am totally against this as a concept. I am into win-win situations, where the patient wins, because they get what they are looking for, and you win because you get the opportunity to deliver the dentistry that you have been trained to do. The closing is one of the reasons why I believe sales has been given a bad name in the past, it certainly can be a sensitive part of the process. However, it is also a very important part of the process and, if you cannot gain patient commitment, then the conversation that you have just had will come to an end.

Let me share a couple of stories to make a point.

A few years ago, my wife asked me if I would go shopping to buy some new furniture for our lounge. We have been living in our house now for 12 years, it is a very old house and during this time, we have slowly been renovating the house. The lounge was the only room we had not bought furniture for.

Now, I hate shopping with a passion and I can't think of anything worse on a day off than walking round shops. So I told her to do all the homework and take me to the one or two shops where she liked the furniture. I was going to have one day off work, but we were going out to buy. I have always taken the view, that if I have to take more than one day off work to shop, then I am losing money.

So off we went on to a shop in Stretford, about 6 miles away from where we live. The unusual thing about this shop is that you have to press a buzzer to get in. Immediately my alarm bell started ringing and the words unique and expensive came to mind. The store had some very unusual pieces and both my wife and I fell in love with a leather suite and a few other bits and pieces. I couldn't believe my luck that, within two hours, a deal had been done with the owner of the shop, and I had the rest of the day to myself. There was only one slight issue, there was a discrepancy over the measurements of the settee as the one he showed us was too big for our lounge. The owner stated that they manufactured this leather suite and that they would make it for us and he asked me for the measurements. Unfortunately, I did not have them to hand, so the owner told us to go home and measure up and ring them through to us later on. I said to him, so what happens now and he said go home, measure up and ring the measurements through. So we did exactly as he said.

Unfortunately for me, my wife then said the following words, and you men reading this, have probably heard this before: "As we have time, let me show you the other suite as the other shop is only five minutes away in the Centre of Manchester". So off we went, and, in fairness to my wife, the other shop had some beautiful pieces and the shop assistant was very enthusiastic and she struck up excellent rapport with us. Within ten minutes she had moved all the furniture in her shop and created a new lounge and she rolled down this rug and I was sold. She even had a fire place in the shop similar to the one at home. We struck a deal, except this time; the cost was going to be a £1,000 more than the first shop.

However, again the suite would have been too big and I shared with the girl my concerns, she then stated that she would come round to our house and measure up, so that when the suite was manufactured, it would fit perfectly in the room. We were delighted with the service that she gave and, when she asked me to complete some paperwork and for a deposit of £1,000, it was not a problem. We bought the suite from the second shop. Why? Because the sales assistant simply completed the sale, whereas the sales assistant in the first shop told me to go home and measure up myself. He lost control of the purchase.

In the first chapter, I wrote about when I visited a gymnasium and the reception team would not show me around the gym as it was not company policy, they had designated sales people and I had to come back at 10am. It was my wife's idea to visit this new gym as she thought it would be good to join as a family.

Well, I went back and visited the gym and was shown around by a very enthusiastic girl who gave me a first class tour of the gym. During our walk round, I commented that the gym had excellent facilities and that my kids would love the pool and some of the classes they had. At the end of our show around, she took me into the sales room, where she asked what I thought of the place. I was very complimentary about the gym and the facilities. The conversation then went like this:

S: Membership just for you Mr Latter would be £36 per month.

AL: No, I want a family membership for me, my wife and my two children.

S: That works out at £77 per month.

AL:. Is that all? To be honest I thought it would be more than that.

S: It's good isn't it?

AL: Yes it is, but if I paid for it all at once, do I get a discount?

S: Yes, you save two months, so the payment would work out at £770 per year total membership for you all. That is good, isn't it?

S: Yes, it is very good value. If you like it, then all you need to do is take these forms and discuss it with your wife.

AL: I will do

That is exactly what I did. I went home to discuss it with my wife, who, by the way, had changed her mind, so we never did join the gym, although, to be honest, if she hadn't, we probably would have joined. Do you ever find yourself saying to a patient: here is your treatment plan, why don't you go away and think about it? What typically happens? They probably go home and think about it, just like the gym example.

I believe there are many obstacles to closing and why dentists in particular find this part of the sales process challenging. Here is my take on this topic.

### 1. Fear of rejection

Maybe one of the reasons why we don't ask is because we fear that the patient might say no. If we receive a no, then that might make us feel uncomfortable. You have invested all that time into the relationship and you do not want to say anything that might put the patient off. Rather than risking the displeasure of the patient, it easy for you to say, take it home and think about it.

### 2. Don't know how to ask

At dental school, how much of your time was being taught communication and gaining commitment skills? Probably not very much and hence you may not be aware how to ask, or what to say or even what to do next. This is totally understandable.

### 3. Don't want to sound pushy

You don't want to come across as the pushy dentist or sales person by asking.

### 4. We have to give them time to think about it

Another reason I often hear is that we have to give the patient all the options and then give them time to digest them.

### 5. I always want time to think about it

I am generalising here, but having worked with thousands of dentists during the last 18 years, I find dentists in particular are slow decision makers. I believe this may be because you like to do a lot of research on a product before you buy it. I am devoting a whole section to this topic later on in this book. However, if you like to do a lot of research and require lots of information before you buy something, my belief is that you feel that the patient needs to do the same. Hence that might be one of the reasons why dentists bombard the patient with lots of information and give them plans and tell them to go away to think about it.

As I have mentioned before, I am not into hard sales closing techniques and using unscrupulous tactics to get patients to buy things. I am totally against it and it makes me feel uncomfortable. I would not push a person to come on one of my programmes, if I did not think they would benefit more than me, as I soon would gain a bad reputation and my good name means a lot to me.

However, if you don't gain commitment to the treatment plan, then it does not matter how good your clinical skills are, you will never get a chance to put them into practice and no one benefits at all. The principle of asking goes back to the biblical times. 'Ask and ye shall receive'. Everybody knows it, if you don't ask you don't get, but in real life it very rarely gets practiced.

If you become a really attentive listener, then you will very quickly pick up signals from your patients which demonstrate their interest in your services. These are called buying signals.

## Buying Signals

A buying signal indicates that the patient is interested in your services. It can either be verbal, or non- verbal. If you listen very carefully, there are real indicators that the patient wants to proceed with your plan.

Let's look at the gymnasium story. I gave the sales girls several buying signals during her presentation. Did you pick any of these up? They included:

My kids would love this pool.

When she quoted the price, I said that I thought it would be more than that.

I asked if I paid all at once whether I'd get a discount.

In the first furniture shop, I asked the owner, what happens now when we were discussing measurements. I was ready to buy and he told me to go home and take the measurements myself.

Here are some of the things that your patients might say during the consultation:

When can we start?

Does it hurt or is it painful?

How much is the treatment?

How long does it take?

What will the end result look like?

Will it be ready for my wedding?

These can be all classed as signals that the client wants to proceed and is genuinely interested in your treatment. So please listen carefully to buying signals. This is the main advantage of having a pro-active nurse working with you.

If you get these signals, then ask a simple question, the test close (see Chapter Four), such as:

Mrs Patient, how does this sound?

Is this what you are looking for?

If you get a positive response, then you are ready to move to the next stage in the process which is gaining commitment.

Here are some examples of closing:

## Just Ask
This is when you do exactly what is says on the tin. You ask your patient if they want to go ahead with the treatment.

Would you like to proceed?

Would you like to go ahead?

## Alternative Close
This is when you give the patient two alternatives to choose from and whichever they choose means they are going ahead with one of them. For example:

Would you like morning or afternoon appointments?

Did you want to pay it all at once, or spread the payments over six months?

Did you want to start the treatment before your holiday or after?

If they choose one, then they are committing to the treatment.

## Next Step Method
This is where you are assuming that the patient wants to go ahead, or you are 99% certain, and then you ask the patient to take the next step, whatever that it is. It could be:

If you are happy to go ahead, all we now need to do is walk to the desk to make those appointments?

If you are happy to go ahead, Mrs Patient, then we just need to take some impressions, is that okay with you?

Hopefully you will get a positive response and you can move to the commitment

## Opportunity Method

The opportunity method is when you have a window of opportunity for the patient that will hopefully get them to take action. Examples of the opportunity method are:

Mrs Patient, I have some good news for you, we have had a patient re-schedule their appointment, we can take the impressions now.

Mrs Patient, I don't know if you are aware, but we have 50% off teeth whitening on Wednesdays so the price will be £249 as opposed to £498.

Hopefully your suggestion will excite the patient into taking action. Notice I never said cancelled, but re-scheduled. I believe the word cancelled is a negative word, where re-scheduled is more positive. I personally would ban the word cancelled in your practice.

Another question I get asked is what happens if the wife needs to discuss it with the husband or vice versa. There are three strategies you can employ here:

1. You can follow up with the client with a telephone call at home.

2. You can suggest an appointment for both of them to come in together, so that you can answer any questions the other party may have.

3. You could suggest that they make an appointment, because you are very busy and, if they decide to cancel, then suggest that the patient can ring the next day.

I personally like number two or three, as at least you are in full control of the situation.

When I have coached my delegates on my courses, this part of the programme has brought about spectacular results, beyond their wildest dreams. I have had clients who have gone back to their practice the next day and talked about treatment options with their clients and, instead of telling them to go away and think about it, they have asked if they want to proceed. It is incredible how many people have said yes, they would be delighted to go ahead. The results have been truly amazing.

I remember one orthodontist from London telling me that he kept records and in the previous month before my course, he had a 2 in 13 closure rate. The following month this went up to 11 out of 14 private cases, all because he asked the patient for commitment. I have had specialists tell me that, by asking the patient if they want to go ahead, they have increased their business by 30%.

I am not saying closing is easy, it isn't. There are going to be times when you have discussed with a patient a complex treatment plan with various options, costs and time issues and it is appropriate for the client to digest this information and give the patient time to think about your suggestions. However, make another appointment with the patient to come back and visit you and therefore you can discuss any issues and hopefully you can gain patient commitment. At the very least, you are in full control of the consultation.

Don't forget, if you take the c out of close, it spells lose. You lose, the patient loses, everyone in your practice loses.

## Things to do

1. Listen attentively to buying signals. These are indicators that the patient is keen to proceed.
2. Get into the habit of using test closes, 'how does that sound?' is my favourite one.
3. Ask for commitment using one of the methods above, the worst that can happen is they say no.

Chapter Eight:

# Analysing Your Patient's Personality Style

Have you ever considered when selling your services to a patient, what type of personality style they have? In my opinion, one area that is important when communicating to your patients is to consider their personality style. In fact, it can be absolutely crucial, because if you want to be able to influence somebody to take on board your ideas, then you might have to adopt a different approach depending on the personality style of the person you are speaking to. What will work with one person does not necessarily work with someone else. Let's therefore look at some personality styles of patients that might come into your practice. Please bear with me, because I am going to contradict a few things I have written in earlier chapters, but I hope you will understand why.

If you look at people's personality styles they probably fit into four categories. These are **pragmatic, extrovert, amiable/ passive** and **technical**. Let's look at the characteristics of each one of these in a light-humoured way.

## Pragmatic
Typically pragmatic people are time-conscious people who probably don't like too much chit-chat, which contradicts some of the things I have been discussing in previous

chapters. They are very business-like and hence they might not want to build rapport. They want to come to the dentist and be in and out as quickly as possible. They may be in a position of leadership, possibly a manager, or a director of their own business and with them, time is money. They don't like detail and want things explained in layman's terms quickly, without any fuss. These are the type of people who don't like holidays, they cannot sit around on a beach all day as they get bored quickly. Within a day, they are organising football games and competitions. They often have short attention spans and probably don't like watching sport. The thought of sitting for 90 minutes watching a football game, or even longer for a cricket match, is not on their agenda. They can be very competitive and love squash, tennis etc. They want to get things done quickly and they also make decisions quickly. Once they make a decision, they stick with it and they want to get on with it. Think now of somebody who you know who might be pragmatic?

## Extrovert

Extroverts are probably in some sort of sales role or PR, or a job where they are talking to people all day, for example a hairdresser. They like to be around people and are usually good company. You might know people that when they walk in a room, it lights up, these are often extroverts. People like being around extroverts, they are fun. They will probably love going to sporting events and they cheer the loudest if their team scores. You are not likely to see extroverts at the canal fishing; they will just get bored after ten minutes. At a drop of a hat they will travel 300 miles to watch their favourite team, or to an event or concert. They like to spend time building rapport with people and they also love competitive sports and games, which they will want to win. Like pragmatics, they will make a decision very quickly but then they want something yesterday. Like pragmatics, they don't need a lot of information and don't like detail. If you do a good job for extroverts, then ask them for referrals, because they will know other extroverts and they will help you with more of the right type of patients. They will love you for life and can really help your business.

## Passive

The third personality type are amiable or passive people. They are likely to be the quieter type of person, timid, but friendly. They like to please. They might be in an administrative position, usually a role where there is not a lot of pressure and they don't need to make rash or quick decisions. In fact, they probably won't be in a role where they need to make decisions at all, because they don't want to upset people. They probably exist in some parts of the civil service as it is a safe job for life, good pension and flexible. They have probably been living in the same area all their life and driving the same car, as they won't like the hard-faced car salesman putting pressure on them to make a purchase. They are nice people and think of other people a lot. They are the type of people that you will see fishing, because it gives them time to think. They love thinking. You also see them in the middle lane of the motorway, as the inside lane has all those nasty lorries and the outside lane is too fast. Sitting in the middle lane of the motorway driving at 55mph is safe.

Passive people are slow decision makers and they certainly will not like to be rushed. You have to spend time getting to know them as a person and building rapport will be an important part of the process. If they feel that you have not got their best interest at heart, they will go the other way and you will lose a good client. They have to feel comfortable with you.

Last, but not least, are the technical patients.

## Technical

You will spot the technical people a mile away. They may wear glasses and be in some sort of technical job i.e. dentists, accountants, teachers or some sort of engineering job. They dress conservatively, certainly not flash and not labels. They will probably have the latest gadget, such as the latest iPod Touch or Smartphone. They would have queued all night for the iPad. If you ask the technical person the time, they will tell you the time in the UK and then the time in every other continent. Ask them the temperature in the car, they will give you it in Centigrade and Fahrenheit, and the weather for the next three days. They love information and will have pie charts all over their offices. They will know to a penny what they spend on their mobile telephone, gas, electricity, and they will have all the website addresses where you can save money. Technical people love information and research and because of this they are slow decision makers. I talk about this on my courses and it is amazing how many dentists agree with me and how their team members all start laughing. I have heard stories of an orthodontist who openly admitted that he visited 12 shops to buy a rucksack, or a dentist who travelled 14 miles to buy grass seed for his garden, so that he could save a few pennies per bag. He also informed the group that he did four hours research on the internet to establish this information.

So that is a light hearted look at the four categories that people fall into. So why is this important? Mainly because you are going to have to change your style to suit the person you are dealing with.

If you are talking to an extrovert, then you will need to be enthusiastic about the end results. For example, if they are interested in teeth whitening, then be excited for them about how they will look and how it will help them in their job. Show them before and after pictures, and they will be excited about testimonial letters. If you are excited, they will probably be, and, as I have already mentioned, they will make a quick decision, probably based on emotion. When they do say yes, shut up and either book the next appointment, or get on with the procedure there and then. Do not give technical information to extroverts, you will not only lose them, but also you will bore them at the same time.

I find pragmatics make decisions based on logic. They will weigh things up, such as the costs versus the benefits of the procedure. They are fast decision makers and, like extroverts, do not like detail. These people are very time management orientated and will probably not want to miss working time, so you will make a pragmatic person delighted if you can do early starts, lunchtime or evening appointments. Please mention this when you are selling your services, it could be a clincher and also they might pay for this. They might want to negotiate, as they like to get some sort of a deal, so beware and be prepared.

In my opinion technical people also buy on logic. They are not emotional people and they will probably not like the enthusiastic approach. What they do like however is information, and they will love charts, statistics and background information. I once spoke to a dentist who told me that he was once selling an implant procedure and the patient, who was a finance director, could not get enough information. He wanted to know everything. Do not rush these people, they do like to consider options and of course they like to weigh things up. Last thing, when quoting prices, please be precise to the final figure, including the pennies.

In my opinion amiable people buy on emotion and the feel-good factor will be important to them. They will want to know that their teeth will be with them when they reach a hundred. They will probably want their hand holding and a lot of re-assurance will be important. However, again like technical people, they will not want to be rushed. They are naturally slow decision makers. They will have to feel that you have their best interests at heart and that you care about them. You have to spend time building rapport with amiable people and also ensure that your nurse is with you at all times. They can be vital here, especially walking the patient to the desk, as they are likely to either change their mind, or ask the nurse another question. They want re-assuring and to feel safe. However, if they do like you and you do a great job for them, don't be surprised if you get a nice bottle of wine, or chocolates at Christmas. They will remember you and they will be very loyal to your practice. They will not want to change. If you are considering an insurance scheme, then spend time re-assuring these patients that it is in their best interest and that it will benefit them in the long run. Don't expect a letter to do the trick.

A question I often get asked is how quickly can you find out who fits into which category? Why not start doing this with your team; it's a great exercise to do. Discuss the different styles and then go round the room and see who fits in where. You will have a lot of fun and you will also start to see which group some of your patients fit in. In general, through practice, you can very quickly find out within just a few minutes of meeting someone where they fit in, and also how you then need to adapt your style towards them.

Is this important? The longer I am in the business of working with people, the more I believe this is crucial. If I look back at some of my failures in sales, it was because I didn't consider the personality type of the person who I was trying to build a relationship with. I also urge you to consider if someone has said no to you, when it should have been a yes, consider if it was your presentation style towards this person. Maybe you rushed when you should have taken time, or maybe you bombarded a pragmatist with too much technical information. Maybe you didn't spend time considering the style of that person.

## Things to do

1. Ensure that your whole team read this material and for a bit of fun, in a team meeting, go round the room and discuss each person's personality style

2. Consider your patients personality style when communicating with them and most importantly adapt and change your own style if necessary.

Chapter Nine:

# Following up to Provide
# World Class Customer Care

In 1997 I ran a sales programme in Manchester and I had a mixture of delegates from all sorts of industries. We had sales people from radio, IT people, hoteliers and two dentists. When I first found out that there were two dentists taking my course, I was racking my brains to try and understand why they were taking a sales course with me. After interviewing them both in detail, I quickly discovered that they both had spent thousands of pounds developing their dental technical skills, but they were not very good at communicating their ideas and getting patients to buy into their skills.

Compared to the other delegates, they were quite reserved and shy and, to be honest, I was not sure if they enjoyed the programme, or if they had actually benefitted from participation. So, about a month after taking my programme, I decided to give them both a ring at home just to find out. I wasn't looking forward to the telephone call as I was expecting not to hear good news. However, nothing could have been further from the truth and all I heard was success after success. They told me that:

1.  Their uptake of treatment had increased

2. They both felt more confident talking money and dealing with patient objections
3. They had built better and stronger relationships with their patients and were now receiving more referrals
4. They had a more positive attitude about the future

They both stated that they wanted to do the course again and in addition, they had friends they wanted to do the programme as well. From these conversations, six months later I ended up delivering a two-day Ethical Sales & Communication Programme in Oxford to 27 dentists and their team members. The rest is history! Over the last 18 years, I have now delivered this particular programme to over 8,000 delegates. In a typical year, I run 12 open courses and around ten in-house courses, where I visit the practice to deliver my coaching. During this time, I have spoken at every major dental conference in the country, Ireland and now Europe and I have had a book published on communication skills. During this time, I probably spent the best part of £7,000 on advertising. So why am I sharing this with you? I often wonder what would have happened if I had not rung Barry and Neil and followed up with them. In fact, I can safely say that the above might not have happened.

On a side issue, my relationship with Neil has gone from strength to strength and we are now very good friends and both our families have been on holiday together. Neil is now a Clinical Director at the Oasis Dental Practice and specialises in fitting implants.

There have been many advantages of following up with my two dentists all those years ago.

On the other side of the coin, as I am delivering all these programmes, I am a big spender with hotels. On average I spend £20,000 a year on hotels, with accommodation on top. As I am writing this book, I have been a Business Coach for 23 years, so it is safe to say I have spent a lot of money on hotel facilities. I can only recall once in 23 years, somebody ringing me up after my programme to see if everything was okay and to thank me for using their facilities. Occasionally I might receive a feedback form to complete electronically, which I have never been bothered to complete.

If somebody followed up and spoke with me and asked more questions to find out about my business, there is a very good chance that they might build a relationship with me and win ongoing business. I have never really built any loyalty to a brand or a hotel.

In fact, I cannot recall anybody ringing me up from a garage after purchasing a car, it very rarely happens.

There are many advantages of following up with your clients.

These include

1. Your clients will love the fact that you have followed up.
2. Because your clients will be delighted that you have contacted them, they will tell their friends, relatives and work colleagues which will mean

that you will build a pipeline of the right types
of referrals to your door.

3. You will learn if the client is okay or not, or
   has any problems or issues. It is better that
   they tell you and not their friends.

So why it is very few businesses in the UK follow up when
you purchase a product or service?

I am not sure. I think that people do not see the benefits
of doing so. Once a sale has been made, then they are on
to the next one. They don't see the benefits of long term
relationships and what future opportunities can be created.
This is a shame, because all of a sudden the relationships has
come to an end. So, if you do have some sort of follow up
process within your practice, you will stand out from the
crowd and truly become world class.

So my question to you is this, do you follow up with your
patients after they have visited you?

Now it might be impossible to follow up with every client
and if a client is coming in for orthodontic treatment and you
ring them after every appointment, it might lose the effect.
However, what if you followed up with, say, six patients
a day by giving the patient a ring at home just to see if
they were okay, especially after a difficult procedure? What
difference do you feel that would make to your practice and
ongoing relationships?

If you run an orthodontic practice, make a special event of
'debond' day. Here is a patient who has worn your braces
for several months and you are now taking them off, make a

fuss of them. I know some practices who the give the parents a small gift for the trouble they have taken bringing their child to the practice. You could also perhaps give the child a small gift, perhaps for not breaking their brace. If you are a specialist, you could give a detailed report back to your referring dentist on the treatment you have administered to their patient. Again, it creates value and shows that you have genuinely cared for their patient.

If you don't already do this, I urge you to meet with your team and consider what you can do to follow up with your patients and start putting a programme in place. There are so many advantages in doing so and of course you will stand out.

## Things to do

1. Speak with your team and discuss how you can follow up with your patients, if you don't already do so.
2. Discuss a time when you were followed up by a shop or organisation when you made a purchase. How did you feel? Has it ever happened?
3. Measure the impact and share your experiences with your team.

Chapter Ten:

# Dealing with Customers'
# Complaints

<u>(This is what happens when you deal it with badly)</u>

I am tired, I am irritable and all I want to do is go to my bed. You must have experienced this feeling?

I have just driven down from Manchester to a hotel in Bristol and I have been in the car for five hours and it is now 10.30pm. Now this hotel is a typical old Georgian English hotel surrounded by large similar buildings and from the outside it looks warm, inviting and I am excited about my bed.

From here you think it's easy, but on the contrary this is where all my problems begin. You see the hotel's car park is a private road at the back of the hotel which slopes downwards which I started to drive down. This is where the fun really started, I am driving down this road and there are no spaces and cars parked either side of the road and, when I finally got to the bottom of this long road, there is nowhere to turn my car round. I am now stuck. I had to start driving up the hill, backwards, in the dark, trying my hardest to avoid the parked cars. It was a nightmare and it took over 20 minutes to get to the top. After a further 20 minutes I finally found a parking space on the street. However there is the worst smell from my car, as you can imagine, and I believe I have burnt my clutch.

I duly complain to the reception staff and receive zero sympathy and no apology. I might as well have talked to the wall.

The next day all my fears came true. In fact I could still smell my car on the street and I need a new clutch. I contacted my recovery company and it is so bad that I had to be towed home from Bristol back to Manchester and I missed a concert on the Friday night. I am annoyed and frustrated.

After taking my car into the garage to be told it will probably cost £1,400 to repair it, I decided to write an email of complaint to the hotel management. Please let me say at this stage, I am not looking in any way for a contribution to my repairs, I know it isn't going to happen. All I want is for them to write back, or call me, and tell me they are:

1. Sorry, show me some sympathy
2. Tell me that they will make some changes, so that is doesn't happen to anyone else.

Now think about it. If this was your business, what would you do? Is it:

a. Ring the client immediately at home and apologise
b. Send an email within a few hours again apologising

> c. Or wait five days and write an email and only apologise on the fifth paragraph and show zero sympathy.

Yes, you've got it, c is the correct answer. Here is the hotel's reply.

Dear Mr Latter,

Thank you for your email regarding the use of our car park on Thursday night.

We make it clear to guests wishing to use the parking that it is limited and have an area at the bottom where guests can turn around, we ask guests not to park in this area and it is covered by a motion sensor light.

Sometimes guests/member of the public may end up parking in these areas without authorization and this makes it difficult to turn a vehicle around, in these instances the hotel reception is usually able to track down the owner of the parked vehicle and ask them to move it.

I'm sorry that you experienced issues in manoeuvring your car out of the car park and I will review your feedback accordingly.

Kind regards

(I have taken the persons name out)

General Manager

I could not believe it. Normally I am quite a placid person and I would put things like this behind me. I was so appalled about what happened and the response I received, that I then spent the next hour on Trip Advisor writing shocking feedback about the hotel. I have to say this is totally out of character, as I normally could not be bothered. However, I was so annoyed with their response that it had this effect on my actions.

I personally don't mind the odd complaint in my business, as long as we don't get many. The reason why I like complaints is that it gives you the opportunity to become a hero. If you go above the call of duty in dealing with a complaint, you can recruit raving fans for your business/practice. I recently delivered some coaching to an engineering company in Lancashire who received a few complaints from a customer based in Ireland. I told him to go and visit the customer, iron these difficulties out and go above the call of duty. The result was a new relationship and an increase in orders.

When you deal with a customer issue well, you can become a star and the customer respects and values you. When you deal with it badly, then you lose a customer. They also tell 8,540 people - that is how many are on my mailing list.

It is so important to your practice that you deal with complaints immediately and also that you go the extra mile. With social media and the role of the internet, if you have a bad experience, you can inform the whole world within seconds.

I honestly believe that, however good you may be at the patient journey and customer service, you are going to get the odd mistake in your practice. Here are a few steps you can take to address the issue and ensure that you recruit raving fans for your practice.

1. First of all, put yourself in your patient's shoes. You have to see things from their point of view. If you have made a mistake, let's see what impact the mistake has had on them. You cannot do anything unless you walk in your patient's shoes

2. Say you are sorry, and say it quickly (not in the fifth paragraph). Don't forget, your patient is upset and not happy and a sincere apology will go long way to reducing their anger and frustration.

3. Tell the patient that if you were them you would feel the same way. Show real empathy here, understanding what impact your mistake would have on you personally.

4. Address the issue and put your wrong right, but go above the call of duty. I often call this as ABCD. In other words, do more than the patient expects. If you do this then you can become a hero and your patients will love it.

5. Ensure that you follow up with your patient to make certain that everything is okay and that they are happy now.

Example

I would like to share an experience that happened to me last year with a hotel in Dublin which illustrates what happens if you don't address the issue properly.

I was running one of my two-day courses at a well known brand hotel that I use all the time. Because I was travelling by plane, I shipped all my manuals and books and they left England in two boxes. I contacted the hotel a few days later and, to my surprise, they informed me that they had only received one of the boxes. I waited a few days and rang the hotel again only to receive the same response. I could not believe it. As the programme was only a few days away, and because I had run out of my own books, I could not give the delegates a copy of my book. As this was my first programme in Ireland, this was not the impression I wanted to make.

After the programme, I came back to England and sent a book to each delegate with an apology. I decided to make a claim for the loss of my books, which totalled £350. I also asked the Post Office to investigate and could not believe their report.

They confirmed that, in fact, both boxes had arrived. I was furious.

I contacted the hotel to inform them and I also shared with them the name of the person who signed for my boxes. After they conducted their own investigation, they found the other box and, as I expected, the hotel representative apologised and said she would send the boxes back. She then went on to say that she would give me a 15% discount on further bookings at the hotel. I could not believe what she said. Here is a hotel who lost one of my boxes, denied they had in fact received it with the result that, on my first programme in Ireland, I could not give the delegates all the appropriate supplies. All the hotel was offering me was a small discount on future bookings. I told the hotel representative the problems she had caused me and the expense and time of having to send the books individually to each delegate after the course. I asked her if she were me, would she hold another course at the hotel. To be honest, I was surprised by her lack of empathy. It was obvious she did not see things from my point of view. I felt she was trying to fob me off. After a few heated words and discussions, she finally knocked a considerable amount off the bill and a 50% discount off any future booking with the hotel, which I accepted.

As I am writing this book, I have just completed a second programme in this Dublin hotel. It was excellent and a better experience than the first one. It is amazing how customer service improves in a recession. Do you find people try harder?

I believe complaints are good for your business and are not the end of the world. It is impossible to get it right all the time. However, ensure that if you do upset your customer, really see things from their point of view and act quickly. Go above the call of duty and give the patient more than they expect, then you can make a friend for life and a superb ambassador for your practice.

## Things to do
1. Please re-read these case studies again and learn from them.
2. Think about a time you had a complaint handled well, what happened and how it made you feel.

3. Always see things from the patient's point of view. If you don't, you will not be able to handle the complaint well.
4. Give your team members flexibility and give them the authority to put a wrong right. Even give them a small budget to cover any costs that they might incur.
5. Discuss in your team meetings if there is a breakdown in a system or procedure. Change it, so that you eliminate complaints.

You have arrived!

Enrica, Me, Martina

# Ashley Latter

Ashley started his working life as a Trainer with the internationally acclaimed Dale Carnegie Training Organisation. He had three roles with them, firstly selling and promoting the courses in Manchester, delivering the programmes and he was also an International Master Sales Trainer, this meant he went round the world training the trainers. This is the highest award that can be given to a Dale Carnegie Careerist.

In 1997 two dentists Neal Sampson and Barry Oulton, together with 15 sales people from other industries took Ashley's course in Manchester. Due to their success, Ashley has now delivered his programme to over 8,000 dentists worldwide. An added bonus is that Neal is today is one of Ashley's best friends and their families have enjoyed holidays together both in the UK and abroad.

The Ethical Sales and Communication programme is legendary in the UK Dental world and is probably the most sought after programme in dentistry today. Ashley has delivered it in 14 different countries, including Estonia, Serbia Canada and five times in the USA.

Apart from the Ethical Sales and Communication course, Ashley delivers other programmes including The Advanced Ethical Sales and Communication Programme, Creating a World Class Patient Journey, Public Speaking Course for Beginners, A Reception Programme - How to Turn Telephone Enquiries into Appointments and his Life Skills Boot camp, which is a kids course where he teaches 16-24 year olds skills to help them sell themselves better in interviews, develop extra self-confidence and a more positive attitude.

Ashley also works with a very forward thinking group of dentists and orthodontists on the Serious Players Club, which is an Entrepreneur group. Ashley is the author of several books including; **Helping patients to say YES, Don't Wait for the Tooth Fairy - How to communicate**

**effectively and create the Perfect Patient Journey** and **You are worth it - Communicate your fees with self-confidence and achieve the income your services deserve.** He wrote a chapter in Dental Masters and has written and published hundreds of articles.

In 2014, Ashley was voted number 12 in top 150 most influential people in UK Dentistry and he was one of two only overseas speakers to present at the 100th Dutch Dental Conference, which was opened by the King of Holland.

Ashley has delivered over 23,000 hours of business coaching to the dental industry all over the world. Simply, he is the best at empowering dentists and their teams to communicate with their patients, which results in a world class patient journey, more patients saying YES to treatment plans and increased profits for their practices. During the last 18 years, working with his clients and by tracking their results, he has helped them communicate and sell over £200m worth of extra dental treatment in an ethical way world-wide.

When he is not delivering presentations (over 140 in 2014), he has an extremely busy personal life. He is married to Graziella, with two daughters Enrica and Martina. He has lived in Manchester all his life. In any spare time he has, he enjoys keeping fit, walking with his family in the Lake District, going to concerts and loves reading personal development books, over 25 books a year. He has run three marathons raising money for cancer research and has also delivered his programmes a few times for charity, mainly Bridge2Aid. He is a passionate Manchester United supporter, and has had a season ticket at Old Trafford for over 40 years.

# Ashley's Courses and Products

Ashley provides a range of services including:

## ETHICAL SALES AND COMMUNICATION PROGRAMME FOR DENTISTS, ORTHODONTISTS, CLINICAL DENTAL TECHNICIANS AND TREATMENT COORDINATORS

Over 8,000 dentists and their teams have taken part on this unique two-day programme which ultimately helps dentists, orthodontists and their teams improve their uptake of treatment plans, achieve the prices their services deserve and deal confidently with patient objections. Many dentists often report back on developing new skills, increased self-confidence and a life-changing experience. Ashley often gets quoted from the dental profession that they wished they had met him straight after Medical School.

*"You don't know what you don't know until you've seen and heard it…Take the plunge, you won't regret it and it will pay for itself. The week after I booked in over £20k of new implant treatments"*

**Andy Denny, Cosmetic Dentist, Twenty 2 Dental**

## ADVANCED ETHICAL SALES PROGRAMME

A world class, one day programme designed to refresh and advance your ethical sales skills to make you the most powerful communicator and further increase your self-confidence, enabling you to influence and sell with ease and integrity

*"The more I take your programme, the more I learn and discover new concepts I previously missed. I have taken your programme five times in the last four years, it is not surprising that my treatment plan acceptance has increased year on year over these years"*

**Stephen Jacobs Owner of Dental FX**

## ONE DAY RECEPTION PROGRAMME

Dental Practices spend thousands of pounds each year marketing and attracting leads to their practice. Each lead needs to be treated correctly to ensure that the patient enquiry turns into an appointment, and ultimately a client. This becomes even more important as patients are shopping around for their treatment and practices are becoming less reliant on the National Health Service. If a patient stays as a patient with you for 10 years and they join a membership plan, then they could be potentially worth more than £5000 to you.

**"***Thoroughly enjoyed the course last Thursday, please let Ashley and Alistair know our girls have signed up several new patients this week already - they are far more confident at talking with patients over the phones"*

**Giles Ratcliffe, Milnsbridge Dental Practice, Grange Dene Dental Practice**

## PRACTICE MANAGERS LEADERSHIP AND COACHING PROGRAMME

Wouldn't it be great if every team member did exactly what they were supposed to do, in exactly the right way? And even better, if every team member went the extra mile' for the practice every day. Well, some practice owners can achieve this happy state, but it takes a great deal of focus, and some great people management skills which you will learn on this course to make it happen.

## SPEAKING AT CONFERENCES

Ashley's presentations are for people and companies who are looking for ideas, techniques and new information about their everyday situations, problems and challenges, in short, anyone who is looking for ideas that can improve their performance in the workplace. Ashley will personally design a bespoke presentation for your conference.

## IN-HOUSE PROGRAMMES

Ashley designs and delivers in-house training for clients who are looking to make major breakthroughs in their practice. Ashley will listen to you to understand your goals, understand the issues of your team and then deliver a Behaviour Change Programme that will improve the performance of your team. Specialist areas include delivering the Ethical Sales & Communication Programme, Creating a World Class Patient Journey, Transforming Your Marketing and Building a High Performance Team.

[Please note, I turn down more programmes than I deliver. I will only deliver a programme if I know I can achieve a significant return on your investment. I don't do "it will be nice to have Ashley speak to motivate the team" afternoons.]

*"I highly recommend the Ethical Sales and Communication course to anyone looking to increase turnover and profitability in their practice. Over the last 12 months we've had an eight fold increase in the take up of Invisalign treatments. On one open day alone we converted 20 enquiries from patients who actually went into Invisalign treatment. The return on investment has been substantial. Can't recommend it enough"*

**Tirj Gidda, Principal Dentist, Omnia Dental Spa**

## THE SERIOUS PLAYERS CLUB

Ashley coaches a select group of dentists, orthodontists and entrepreneurs who meet four times a year to develop entrepreneur and business skills. These groups are forward thinkers who want to make major breakthroughs in their practice. They are also open-minded and willing to share best practices and help coach their colleagues to greater success. Besides Ashley coaching and leading the workshop, there is an outside speaker who presents at each meeting. Participants have to be interviewed and accepted by the rest of the group.

*"Having already attending many training sessions with Ashley I was looking for the next step and joined Ashley's Entrepreneur Club. As a result of much of what we introduced, our clinic has just had its most successful year ever and we are looking forward to see what this year will bring"*

**Paul Stone, Specialist Oral Surgeon and Clinical Director**

## SERIOUS PLAYERS CLUB FOR TECHNICIANS

This basically works on the same lines as the other Serious Players Club programmes. Meetings take place every three months and Ashley coaches technicians on transforming their marketing, developing their ethical sales, communication skills, their leadership and business skills.

## PUBLIC SPEAKING FOR BEGINNERS

Learn to present effectively to an audience, groups or even one to one. We use proven techniques to improve your performance and enhance your self-confidence. With group and one-to-one coaching, participants make major breakthroughs in an area that may otherwise seem daunting

*"Despite many years of presenting I had never had much formal training and always felt unsure and insecure about whether I could get my message across effectively. Ashley's course gave me the practical knowledge and self-belief I had always lacked. The real test of this was presenting to 550 dentists at last year's BDA Conference, an experience I was actually able to enjoy!"*

**Andy Lane, Apollonia House Dental & Health Care Ltd**

## LIFE SKILLS BOOTCAMP

Everyone knows how competitive it is in the world today, your children will need a new skill set so that they can stand out against their competition. We have developed a programme to help them develop new skills and attitudes that will help them sell themselves better in interviews and to develop extra self-confidence and a more positive attitude. This programme is open to young adults aged 16-24

*"I've just finished the course with Alistair Mann. It was absolutely brilliant. I feel it will really help me with my communication when I go for job interviews"*
**Jack Sampson, Student at Liverpool University**

If you are interested in any of the above services, then please call Lissa on 0161 724 8728 or email Lissa@ thesellingcoach.com.

For more information on our products and services please visit www.ashleylatter.com.Find us too on Facebook, Twitter, LinkedIn and YouTube

Ashley's Newsletter

Ashley writes an email newsletter which is now read by 8,500 subscribers. This goes out every two weeks and to receive a copy please visit www.ashleylatter.com and you can register on line.

Edwards Brothers Malloy
Thorofare, NJ USA
September 13, 2016